The Faroes
The Faraway Islands

The Faroes

The Faraway Islands

ANTHONY JACKSON

ROBERT HALE · LONDON

To

M.E.E.J.

ISBN 0 7090 4304 X

Robert Hale Limited
Clerkenwell House
Clerkenwell Green
London EC 1 R 0 HT

Set in Linotron Sabon by
Rowland Phototypesetting Limited, Bury St Edmunds, Suffolk
Printed in Great Britain by
St Edmundsbury Press Limited, Bury St Edmunds, Suffolk
and bound by WBC Bookbinders

Contents

List of Illustrations

Plates

Between pages 120 and 121
Landscape

Fámjin
Víðareiði
Feeding sheep
Húsavík
Gjógv
Tórshavn
Tinganes

Between pages 152 and 153
Island Work

Sunday fishing
Sandur
Fuglafjørður
Tórshavn ship-builders
Syðradalur
Fuglafjørður

All photographs by the author.

Maps

Map artwork by Helen Jackson.

Acknowledgements

I could not have written this book without the help of my wife, Maja, and numerous Faroese friends who have put up with our endless enquiries over the last twenty years. We have both spent over twelve months in the Faroes during this time and have witnessed the startling changes that have occurred in this relatively short period. I am also indebted to my daughter, Helen, for making the outline maps. My thanks are also due to the former Social Science Research Council (now the Economic and Social Research Council), the Nuffield Foundation and the University of Edinburgh for providing funds for my many trips to the Faroes over the years and for financial help with my research.

Obviously I have had to rely on sources of information other than that which could be observed at first hand. My thanks go to that excellent source book on the Faroes J. P. Trap's *Danmark: Færøerne* (1968) and to the works of J. P. Joensen, who has written so much on the ethnological history of the Faroes. I have leaned on both their works to provide some of the basic information, given in the first two parts of this book, concerning the physical and historical background of the Faroes.

This is not meant to be a comprehensive and detailed guide-book to the Faroes. For that you should turn to K. Hjaltason's *Færøerne rundt – en guide –* if you are able to read Danish. Things change so fast in the Faroes that it is almost impossible to give an up-to-date account, unless it is revised every year. However, there are many good leaflets in English that give most of the practical information that you will require when you get there.

The Faroese have eight letters in their alphabet different from English (see *Glossary*, for their pronunciation). An important letter to note is the Faroese *edd* – ð that is mute or silent.

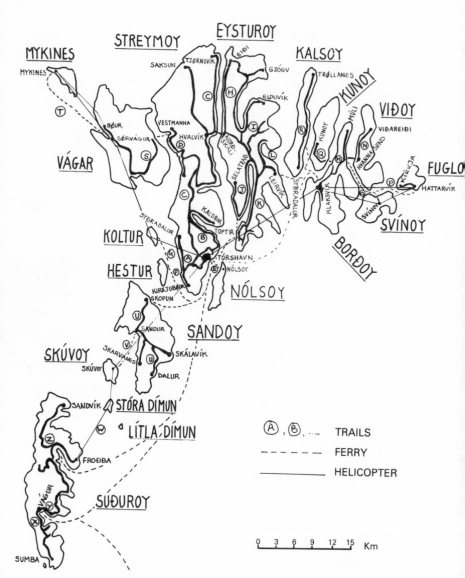

Introduction

At the same distance to the north of Cape Wrath as they are south to Glasgow, lie the Faroe Islands, some 300 km away, yet they are relatively unknown in Britain, except as a vague place mentioned in weather forecasts. Indeed, those most familiar with the Faroes are likely to be either fishermen or service personnel who were stationed there during the war. The poor communications and a dearth of books in English about the Faroes may well account for the general lack of knowledge about these fascinating islands that are Britain's closest neighbours in the North Atlantic.

This book is an attempt to rectify matters by describing some of the natural history of the islands, their social history and present conditions, besides giving a description of all the villages and how to reach them. A chronology of the major events in the Faroes, given in Appendix B, which highlights their historical development up to the present should be referred to periodically.

The historical half partly explains how the Faroese eventually extricated themselves from their nineteenth-century, yet basically medieval, life-style to become one of the most prosperous nations in Europe today. A half-century ago there was only a sprinkling of roads and just a few jetties, whereas today all the villages are linked by road or ferry and there are modern harbours as well as an airport.

Going from village to village, it is noticeable that economic development is by no means equal or even. Some villages still preserve their old-fashioned houses and agricultural methods, while others are modern and full of dynamic activity.

Maps are essential if you want to know where you are. An extremely useful map is the topographical one @ 1:100 000 issued by the *Kort og matrikelstyrelsen* that covers all the Faroes. If you wish for more detailed maps, there is a series @ 1:20 000 in fifty-three sheets. These maps are produced by the Geodætisk Institut, Copenhagen. There is also a 1:8 000 map of Tórshavn available.

Timetables of buses and ferries may be obtained locally or by writing to the Tourist Office in Tórshavn.

A trip to the Faroes is an unforgettable experience, so make the most of it by being prepared.

I THE ANCIENT PAST
(556–1856)

1   First Impressions

Whichever way you approach the Faroe Islands – by air or by sea – they first appear as mere smudges on the horizon that gradually resolve into a series of green, craggy islands as you come closer. When the precipitous cliffs and treeless mountain terrain, covered in verdant grass, become visible, you might spot numerous sheep grazing on the hillsides. On sunny days, the sea becomes blue and the air transparent and startlingly clear, which brings the islands closer together, while small white, woolly clouds form over the peaks. The first human habitations are a delightful kaleidoscope of colours as the walls and roofs of the houses jostle one another in contrasting reds, blues, greens and yellows, besides the prevalent, traditional white and black. As you gaze on these small dwellings that cluster around the bays, you know you have arrived in the faraway Faroes.

Coming by air, you fly over the southern islands before making for the islands' only airport on the western island of Vágar – 'the isle of bays'. Gazing down, you will see the bays and the houses curving round them, while in the centre you may discern the harbour and the church: the twin foci of the community. Around each village you see the cultivated grass fields within the boundary wall, and roads are clearly visible as they snake along the coast or over the hills, joining the villages together. The approach to Vágar airport is an exciting one both physically and mentally. The flight-path takes you either up a long fjord with mountains on either side or up over the sheer cliffs and a long lake to land on the short runway built by the British in the last war. Although not hazardous, the summer months often have sea-fog that can delay the scheduled touch-down, and you may have to circle until a 'window' appears. If you are very unlucky, it might take days before you can land, which is why the Faroes are renowned as 'The Land of Maybe'!

Most air-travellers head for the capital, Tórshavn, 60 km distant. You have the choice of regular buses, taxis or self-drive.

The sea journey to the Faroes is more leisurely and gives you time to adjust to the slower pace of life in the islands. What you will observe is not visible from the air – the thousands of sea-birds, circling, breeding and fishing. You sail between some of these mountainous islands and can see the steep cliffs and breakers, as well as some of the brightly coloured villages that line the bays. Your journey's end is in the heart of Tórshavn – a busy, bustling town down by the harbour. Travelling by sea, you can always take your own car.

The tourist offices are helpful, but tourism is rather under-developed – there are shortages of rooms and eating-places. Hence it is useful to plan your excursions and decide what you want to see. The object of this book is to give you sufficient background information to make the best use of your time, whether you are interested in geology, botany, ornithology, history or a different way of life.

This introductory chapter aims to set out the natural history of the Faroes, since it is the basis of all life here. We begin by looking at the landscape, since this is one of the most attractive features of the Faroes. Yet it needs an explanation of why it is as it is.

The Landscape

The Faroes are a product of continental drift: as America parted company from Europe, it left weaknesses in the earth's crust that allowed the molten magma below to erupt as volcanoes and basalt lava flows. In fact, the Faroe Islands are just the tips of a mountain range of vast basalt sheets that stretch from Ireland to Greenland. Occasional volcanic out-bursts spread layers of reddish ash or tuff on the basalt, and so we find alternating bands of basalt and tuff that are quite visible in the cliff faces today. In periods of quiet volcanic activity, vegetation grew and formed the basis for the coal-seams that are found in the southern islands.

Erosion by ice and rain produced the characteristic north-north-west/south-south-east direction of the fjords and the typical cirques (semi-circular valleys) which characterize the eighteen main islands that constitute the Faroe Islands. They look, altogether, like an inverted triangle and have a total area of 540 sq. m./1,400 sq. km, which is the same as that of their nearest neighbour, Shetland. The coastline is remarkably varied, as it depends on the rock concerned and the amount of erosion. The east and south-east coasts tend to slope down to the water, but the north and west coasts tend to be vertical and form the famous cliffs on which hundreds of thousands of sea-birds breed.

The islands are relatively isolated from any land mass and so are subject to powerful sea-currents. The most important is the Gulf Stream, whose blue, warm and salty waters throw a warm protective shield around the Faroes against the cold, green Arctic currents. The meeting of these two currents is responsible for the depressions forming off Iceland that bring wet and windy weather to northern Europe, besides causing sea-fog in the Faroes during the summer. However, the Arctic current is also important, since it is full of plankton that is the start of the food-chain that sustains marine life around the Faroes.

The major movements of water around the islands are the tides which flow alternately in a north-westerly or south-easterly direction every six hours. Tides affect the currents between the islands, since they change four times a day, and this accounts for the curious movements of ferries as they weave to and from the islands at different times during the day.

The prevailing wind is from the south-west, following the Gulf Stream, and carries rain with it. Rain falls for 70 per cent of the year, and hardly two consecutive days are dry. The average temperature is 11°C in summer but only 4°C in the winter. Cloudy skies are typical, and there are storms. There are enormous differences in local weather, caused by the mountains. The oceanic climate, with the frequent winds, inhibits the growth of trees but promotes emerald-green grass in the summer on which the traditional number of 70,000 sheep graze. Sheep (*får* in Danish) give their name to the Faroes: 'the Sheep Islands'.

At a latitude of 61–2° N and a longitude of 6–7° W, the Faroes get a maximum of 19.5 hours of sunlight in the summer and a corresponding five hours in the winter. In the darker part of the year there are displays of the Aurora Borealis (Northern Lights).

Vegetation

Faroese flora is comparatively recent and stems from the last Ice Age, some 10,000 years ago. It comprises some 350 species each of wild flowers, mosses and lichen and some 600 species each of fungi and microscopic algae. No trees ever grew here, but remains of juniper, dwarf-willow and heather have been found in peat deposits. These species derive from Europe and arrived by accident or design: by wind, currents, birds or man.

Vertical sea-cliffs are covered with algae, while rocks may have crusted lichen on them. Between the tidal areas are wracks, with seaweeds further out to sea. Sandy beaches have various grasses, while pondweeds and algae fill the bottom of lakes. Sedges are found in valley bottoms, and heather and berries higher up. The mountainsides have grassy heathland mixed with grasses, sedges, buttercups and clover. Tops of mountains favour mosses and lichen.

At one time barley was grown, as well as oats, but they never ripened in this damp climate. Today only grass and potatoes are grown agriculturally. Some people grow root-crops besides rhubarb, raspberries and currants. The commonest garden plant is the lupin.

Fauna

The only land fauna found in the Faroes was introduced by man, since no such life-forms survived the last Ice Age. The Norwegian hare was introduced in 1854 for sporting purposes and has multiplied ever since. The Norwegian brown rat came, accidentally, in 1768 on a shipwreck and wiped out the black rat that was here before. The housemouse or fieldmouse came with the early settlers. Only four islands have escaped these vermin.

The Faroes are full of birds: forty species breed there regularly, while some 200 species visit the islands on their migratory journeys. Not surprisingly, the commonest birds are sea-birds, which are to be numbered in millions. The steep cliffs are full of nesting birds during the summer when the seas are full of animal plankton (food for fish and the beginning of the food-chain). When this summer harvest is over, the birds have to fly elsewhere to get their food.

The commonest species is the puffin (*lundi*), which come in April to the cliffs where they build their nests in holes in the turf at the top. They depart with their young at the end of August. Next common are the guillemots (*lomvigi*), which lay their eggs on wide ledges on the cliffs and depart at the end of July. Related, but not so common, are the razorbill (*álka*) and black guillemot (*teisti*). Today an extremely common bird is the fulmar (*havhestur*) but it is a relative newcomer, and its success depended on its driving out other bird-colonies. Related to the fulmar are the Manx Shearwater (*skrápur*), Leach's petrel (*havtyrði*) and the stormy petrel (*drunnhviti*).

Other sea-birds include gannets (*súla*), shag (*skarvur*), kittiwake (*rita*), lesser black-backed gull (*likka*), greater black-backed gull (*svartbakka*), herring gull (*fiskimási*), mew gull (*skatumási*), black-headed gull (*fransaterna*), besides terns (*terna*), the Arctic skua (*kjógvi*), the great skua (*skúgvar*) and eider ducks (*æða*).

There are not so many land-birds, but the best-known and most distinctive is the oyster-catcher (*tjaldur*), which is a national symbol. Speeches are made on the National Flag Day (St Mark's Day, 25 April) welcoming its arrival, although it actually comes in March! Other such birds are the whimbrel (*spógvi*), golden plover (*lógv*), rock pipit (*grátítlingur*), snipe (*myrsnipa*), the wheatear (*steinstólpa*), starlings (*stari*), wrens (*músabródur*), meadow-pipits (*títlingur*), sparrows (*gráspurv*), and a few crows (*kráka*) and ravens (*ravnur*) which survived their proscription. There is only one bird of prey – the merlin (*smyril*).

Marine fauna

The only freshwater fish are salmon, sea-trout, river-trout, char, the three-spined stickleback and the European eel.

Permits are available to fish these species from lakes and rivers.

Many invertebrates living near the shore are essential elements in the food-chain, and they include limpets, periwinkles, dog-whelks, mussels, crabs, sea-urchins, starfish, scallops, cockles, Norwegian lobster, brittle-worms, horse-mussels – all food for fish or man.

The grey seal is the only pelagic fauna that breeds on the coast. The plankton around the Faroes attract both fish and cetaceans. The baleen whales (i.e. plankton-eating cetaceans) gave rise to a profitable whaling industry at one time: the main catches were the fin whale, sei whale and enormous blue whale. Of the toothed whales only the sperm whale was considered worth pursuing, but the smaller bottle-nosed whale and the pilot whale (*grind*) were, and are still, herded and dispatched on the Faroese beaches.

There are some 150 species of fish that are found around the Faroes, but only a handful are thought worth pursuing. Traditionally cod was the most important fish caught, followed by haddock and saithe. What is caught today depends on customer taste and the international quotas in force; it now happens to be blue whiting, cod, saithe, capelin, pout, ocean perch, shrimps, sand-eel and haddock. If these names are unfamiliar, that is because they refer to 'trash fish' which is made into cheap fishmeal and fish-oil for fertilizers. This short-sighted policy of scooping up these small fish which are the food of larger, commercial fish has rebounded on the Faroese, as they are now discovering that there are few fish left in the sea. This foolish interruption of the food-chain has also spelled catastrophe for many species of sea-birds that live on these small fish.

Man is the most recent incomer to the Faroes and had to adjust to the conditions he found there – a poor mineral and soil basis to set up human habitation. If it were not for sea-birds and fish, besides the imported sheep, life would have been impossible. No wonder the population was so small until the nineteenth century! Since then, the human population has sky-rocketed, with consequences on the natural world around them.

2 The Early Settlers and Their Language (556–1056)

Who has not heard of Thule – that Land of Promise and Eternal Youth? The myths surrounding this mystic place hark back more than 2,000 years and are linked to early Greek stories about the mysterious island of Atlantis that lay beyond the Straits of Gibraltar. Yet the Greek geographer Pytheas of Massalia claimed to have visited the areas north of Britain in 330–300 BC and to have reached Thule. It is regrettable that Pytheas' account has been lost and that we have only garbled versions of his explorations. It is not certain that his Thule was indeed Iceland – it could have been Norway or Orkney or Shetland.

Apart from this early, intrepid Greek explorer, the only other seafarers in this part of the world were the Irish Christian missionaries from the fifth century AD onwards. One of the most renowned was St Brendan (484–577) who travelled far and wide on his missionary activities.

These Irish tales of seafaring have to be taken somewhat seriously, since the monks did travel widely. Their boats were *curraghs*, wicker-framed vessels with a hide-covering that are still found today in Ireland. These monks and hermits travelled with oar and sail all around the coasts of Britain, looking for places to set up their refuges. It is only 80 km from Orkney to Shetland and less than 322 km to the Faroes, from there it is but 386 km to Iceland. Even direct from Ireland it is only 966 km to Iceland, while the frequent *fata morgana* (northern mirages) made the distance seem much shorter. Despite such justifiable doubts about Irish tales, these stories have a ring of truth in their descriptions of the places visited, since the monks actually welcomed the barren and desolate areas in the north as ideal places in which to live out the rest of their lives.

As monks are not self-reproducing, they needed replacements, and this must have been done by reinforcements, ferried there by Irish seamen who knew the seas. That this knowledge was widely available is witnessed by the Irish monk Dicuil in his sober account of the islands north of Britain, taken down by word of mouth from priests. This is all recorded in Dicuil's book *Liber de Mensura Orbis Terrae* (*The Measurement of the Earth*) of AD 825. Dicuil was of the most unusual persuasion, at that particular time, believing that the Earth was actually round!

The flavour of his account may be judged from the following extract:

> All round our island of Hibernia there are islands, some small, some tiny. Off the coast of the island of Britain are many islands, some big, some small, some middling; some lie in the sea to the south of Britain, others to the west; but they are most numerous in the north-western sphere and the north . . . There are many other islands in the ocean to the north of Britain which can be reached from the northernmost British Isles in two days' and nights' direct sailing, with full sails and an undropping fair wind. A certain holy man informed me that in two summer days and the night between, sailing in a little boat of two thwarts, he came to land on one of them. Some of these islands are very small; nearly all of them are separated one from the other by narrow sounds. On these islands hermits who have sailed from our Scotia [Ireland] have lived for roughly a hundred years. But, even as they have been constantly uninhabited since the world's beginning, so now, because of Norse pirates, they are empty of anchorites, but full of innumerable sheep and a great many different kinds of seafowl.

The question is whether Dicuil's account substantiates Pytheas' and St Brendan's stories about the travels of Irish monks and others to these islands in the North Atlantic. Is Thule really Iceland and did hermits actually settle in the Faroes? Little archaeological evidence is available to support these claims; only some place-names give credence to the settlement of hermits, such as *papar* names in Iceland and the Faroes. However, pollen-analysis suggests that a change in the vegetation occurred in the period concerned, which could be due to the presence of man.

If Dicuil is to be believed, the Irish discovered the Faroes about the year AD 700 and lived there until they were displaced about 825, when Dicuil was writing his book. We know nothing about the economy of these monks, but presumably they were responsible for the introduction of sheep that were similar to the wild sheep that survived on St Kilda. This stock would have provided milk and wool for the hermits. They must also have been fishermen and probably caught sea-birds. Their numbers could not have been very great, perhaps only a few score.

The 'Norse pirates' – the people who later settled in the Faroes – came mainly from south-west Norway (e.g. Rogaland) and spoke the regional dialect. Traces of this Old Norse tongue are still evident in modern Faroese and bear a marked resemblance to the current speech of south-west Norway.

Half the villages in the Faroes give their names to *víks* (coves), *vágs* (bays) or *fjørds* (fjords) that were probably the primary settlements because of their good landing possibilities. It should be noted that the Faroese do not draw a very sharp distinction between fjords and sounds. Many sounds are named as fjords but not, of course, vice versa. It is interesting to observe that ninety per cent of all *víks*, *vágs*, *fjørds* and *sunds* still contain villages with the same name. Another characteristic feature of Faroese settlements is to build them on an isthmus (*eiði*), as some place-names indicate.

These Norwegian settlers naturally took with them their old customs and traditions. So when they had settled down, they set up *tings* (or 'things') that were assemblies of freemen who met locally to resolve disputes in their districts, according to Norwegian law. Such meetings were presided over by a Law-man (*Løgmaður*), someone who could recite all the laws. Originally six such law-districts existed, but these later became seven sheriffdoms (*syslur*). In addition, there was a plenary session of all the *tings*, the *Alting*, that met annually in Tórshavn. This grand meeting was both a judicial and legislative body that could also act as an executive, thus combining all three arms of government. The Faroese yeomen exercised these powers until 1274, when the Norwegian king Magnus the Lawmender curtailed their rights by reducing the *Alting* to a *Løgting*, just a law-court.

3 The Faroese Saga (*c.* 1000)

The so-called Faroese Saga is not a complete and separate Icelandic saga but a compilation of extracts from other sagas. It was a Dane, C. C. Rafn (1795–1864), the secretary of the *Danish Ancient Text Society*, who ransacked the sagas for details of the exploits of Sigmundur Brestirson and published his findings in 1832, with both Danish and Faroese translations of the Icelandic texts.

As may be imagined, the Faroese Saga is uneven and is not always consistent, because of the way it was put together. The saga really concerns two kinsmen, Tróndur (*c.* 955–1037) and the son of his cousin, Brestir, called Sigmundur (*c.* 970–1005). The main plot relates the struggles between the pagan Tróndur and the Christian Sigmundur for control over the Faroes. It is hardly surprising that the Christian monks who wrote the sagas favoured Sigmundur, despite the bloodthirsty deeds that both heroes committed. In the Faroes, however, the staunchly independent Tróndur is still much preferred to the king's man, Sigmundur.

The saga begins with the bald statement that Grímur Kamban was the first man to colonize the Faroes (*c.* 825) and states that Áud the Deep-minded, on her way to Iceland, gave away Tórstein the Red's daughter, Oluva, in marriage (*c.* 855) and that from her stemmed the leading Faroese family of the day – called Gøtuskegg. A man from Gøta in Eysteroy called Torbjorn but also known as Gøtuskegg (born *c.* 930) – had two sons, Torlak and Tróndur, while his older brother, Sigmund (born *c.* 925), also had two sons, Brestir and Beinir. These two sets of cousins were rivals as to which of them should control the Faroes.

One day the red-haired, freckled and stern-faced young Tróndur went off to Denmark to seek his fortune, although he had inherited the rich farm at Gøta. This adventure resulted in Tróndur's sailing away a very rich man and sets the scene of an unscrupulous man.

Meanwhile the brothers Brestir and Beinir ruled over half the islands and lived on Skúvoy with their mistresses. Each man got a son – they were called Sigmundur and Tóri and who behaved like brothers.

Trouble was brewing, however, down at Hov in Suðeroy where Havgrímur held pagan sacrifices. Two of his men fell to quarrelling over the merits of Brestir and Beinir, versus those of Havgrímur, and so they attacked each other, which resulted in one being killed. The case later came to court at Tinganes but Havgrímur lost face and vowed vengeance on both the brothers. He sought the help of Tróndur, who was very luke-warm about the project, since they were his kinsmen, yet he accepted a tribute from Havgrímur and said that he should also seek help from Tróndur's maternal uncle, Bjarni from Svínoy. Eventually all three men launched an attack on Skúvoy, and Brestir and Beinir were killed – but so was Havgrímur. The two boys, Sigmundur and Tóri, were taken away by Tróndur and later sold to a Norwegian trader as slaves. Tróndur was then left in sole control of the Faroes, but he took the boy Øssur Havgrímson and brought him up for the sake of his dead father.

The two sons of Brestir and Beinir were later released in Norway and took refuge with Torkel (Ulf) Barfrost, who was an outlaw. They stayed with him for six years, until Sigmundur was eighteen and Tóri twenty. In the meantime Sigmundur had made Ulf's daughter, Turid, pregnant, but he promised to marry her when he had made a name for himself.

In the Faroes meanwhile, Øssur Havgrímson had been brought up by Tróndur, and it was decided they should both rule the Faroes between them: Øssur should have the patrimonies of Sigmundur and Tóri in Skúvoy and Stóra Dímun besides the inheritance of his father, Havgrímur, at Hov.

After many war expeditions Sigmundur wished to return to the Faroes, and Earl Håkon reluctantly agreed. When the earl asked him which faith he believed in, Sigmundur replied that he believed only in his own power and strength. The earl said that he himself believed in the goddess Torgerð, and so he took Sigmundur to see her temple. There the earl took a large gold ring from the finger of the priestess and gave it to Sigmundur, saying that he must *never* part from it, on pain of his life.

Sigmundur and Tóri returned to the Faroes but could not reach Gøta to confront Tróndur, so they made their way to Svínoy and raided Bjarni's farm. They spared Bjarni's life because the latter had pleaded clemency for Sigmundur when Havgrímur had killed his father. They then went to Skúvoy and displaced Øssur. A truce was declared between Tróndur and Sigmundur until Earl Håkon could decide the issues between them.

Sigmundur sailed back to Norway, but Tróndur broke his promise to accompany him. The earl then declared that Tróndur owed Sigmundur two sets of blood-money, for the deaths of his father and uncle. On his return to the Faroes, Sigmundur called a *ting* and demanded that Tróndur pay up, but the latter asked for more time to pay. Tróndur also took Leif Øssurson home to Gøta to be brought up. Leif was the son of Øssur Havgrímson.

After King Olaf had been on the throne for two years (i.e. c. 999) he sent for Sigmundur about an important mission. King Olaf had already converted the whole of Trondheim county to Christianity, and he asked Sigmundur to spread this faith to his other dominions.

When he got back to the Faroes, Sigmundur called a *ting* to persuade the Faroese to become Christian but Tróndur and his party resisted. The next year Sigmundur sailed to Eysturoy and cornered Tróndur and forced him to be converted. He then took Tróndur all around the Faroes, and thus he converted the entire population. Sigmundur then tried to take Tróndur to Norway but was twice driven back by bad weather and so gave up the attempt. (There is a hint of witchcraft here.)

When Sigmundur was back in Norway and talking to the king, Olaf demanded Sigmundur's gold ring but the latter refused. The king explained that he wished for the ring only because it would be Sigmundur's bane and he did not want to lose such a faithful servant.

One day when Sigmundur and his followers had gone to

Lítla Dímun to slaughter some sheep, Tróndur and his company arrived, but they were fought off. Later in the summer another attack occurred but again Sigmundur drove them off. In the winter a further attack was made on Skúvoy, where Sigmundur and his family lived. Tróndur was successful this time, and Sigmundur, with his companions, jumped into the sea and attempted to swim to Suðeroy. Only Sigmundur survived, and he collapsed exhausted on a heap of seaweed. Then Torgrímur the Evil, from the village of Sandvík, found the helpless Sigmund and, espying his large gold ring, chopped off his head and took the ring. His body was then secretly buried.

Sigmundur's wife, Turid, became known as 'the Principal Widow' after her husband's death, and she ran the farm on Skúvoy with the aid of her children. Tróndur then suggested to Leif Øssurson that it would be a good idea for him to marry Sigmundur's daughter, Tóra, to put an end to the quarrel between the two families, but she was reluctant to marry Leif.

The mystery of Sigmundur's death remained unsolved, and so Tróndur decided to visit Torgrímur and question him. Torgrímur denied any responsibility but Tróndur had him and his sons manacled while he conjured up the ghosts of the dead. (The sagas constantly suggest that Tróndur dabbled in black magic, as befits a pagan.) When the headless ghost of Sigmundur appeared, Torgrímur broke down and confessed. At the next *ting*, Torgrímur was found guilty of murder and was hanged.

Leif Øssurson eventually got Tóra as his wife, and they set up home in his ancestral place at Hov, so the Faroes were now at peace. Tóralv Sigmundson, Tóra's brother, also married and set up home on Stóra Dímun.

More adventures concerning Leif and his wife Tóra are related, and how Leif killed Sigurdur, the nephew of Tróndur, who was trying to woo Tóra's own mother, the Principal Widow. In this way, Leif achieved vengeance upon the killers of Sigmundur. The news of the death of his nephews so affected Tróndur that he died broken-hearted. Leif then ruled over the entire Faroes, and he and his wife lived on to an old age.

The saga finishes with the bald statement: 'Nothing further

is told of great things happening to Sigmundur Brestirson and his descendants.'

So the saga ends in 1050 – a mere century after its beginning. What is so surprising is that the Faroese figure at all in the Icelandic sagas, because they were really very marginal to Icelandic and Norwegian interests.

While no guarantee can be given that sagas are true, the memories still live on in the Faroes. Thus the so-called Bjarnasteinur, found under the church at Svínoy in 1828, might commemorate the grave of the mediator, Bjarni. It is said that the remains of Tróndur's farm at Gøta are still there. On Skúvoy, Sigmundur's grave-stone and possibly his church's foundations have been discovered in the old burial ground, but even if it is all false, these three names are still kept alive in ballads and stories. This was a glorious moment in the Faroese past – saga or true history makes no difference.

4 The Next 500 Years (1056–1556)

The saga concerning the Faroes is basically about a real struggle of local pagan chiefs, such as Tróndur úr Gøta against the newly Christian followers of the Norwegian king, Olaf Tryggvason. In the event, the Faroes became Christian in the year 1000 – the very year in which the kingdom of Norway slipped from the king's hands and Scandinavia became embroiled in internal wars. A new Olaf subjugated Norway in 1016 – 'St Olaf', for he rooted out paganism in an uncompromising fashion and set about building churches all over Norway. His own downfall was due to the ambitions of the Anglo–Danish king Canute to add Norway to his empire. St Olaf met his death at the battle of Stiklestad on 29 July 1030. His body was taken to the church he had founded at Nidaros – later renamed Trondheim. Stories of miracles associated with him were deliberately spread by the Church and confirmed Olaf as Norway's eternal king'. This cult reached the Faroes, and they adopted him as their patron saint and celebrated the day of his death as their national day: Ólavsøka. Tróndur úr Gøta died in 1035, and his foster-son, Leif Øssurson, received the Faroes as a fiefdom from the Norwegian king Magnus the Good.

In 1268, when the Faroese bishop died and a new one had to be chosen by the canons in Bergen, they selected Erlend, who was both a teacher and a priest in Bergen. Confirmed by the archbishop and installed in 1269, he died in Bergen in 1308. Erlend was to become the most famous bishop in Faroese history. He was well liked in the Faroes, but he made some enemies. Once, when he was in Norway, somebody set fire to the church and the bishop's palace. When he returned, he surveyed the ruins and then doggedly started to rebuild. He was much concerned about the poor state of agriculture and was instrumental in getting the law revised, especially *Seyðabrævið*, 'The Sheep Letter' (1298), that laid down precise rules about the keeping of sheep. Shortly after that, he conceived the idea of building a cathedral in the Faroes at Kirkjubøur; it was begun in 1300 but was never completed because he pressed the people so hard with demands for taxes and labour that they revolted.

During the centuries, the local assembly of freemen, the *Alting*, had developed into a *Løgting*, a local parliament similar to those in Norway, under the elected leadership of the Lawman. In 1273 King Magnus the Lawmender decided that the West Norwegian *Gulating* Law also applied in the Faroes. This resulted in the loss of independence of the *Løgting*, which became simply a law-court, while the Lawman became just a royal official. At the same time, the king promised to send at least two trading vessels to the Faroes each year, with necessary supplies.

Along these trade-routes that spanned the coasts of Europe, on board ship, came the rats that spread the bubonic plague (the Black Death). From the Crimea (1346) via Constantinople to Italy and western Europe (1348) it eventually came to the North Sea and Baltic (1350): between a third and one half of the population died. Both Norway and the Faroes were badly affected; the fall in population drastically reduced the revenue derived from the land, and so the power of the aristocracy diminished. Although the Church was also affected, it continued to take over more and more land until it had control over 40 per cent of the country.

The last Catholic bishop, Amundur Olavsson, was appointed in 1532. This time, it was not the canons of Bergen who decided but the Faroese themselves. In 1536 the Norwegian Council of the Realm was abolished, so both Norway and the Faroes were thenceforth ruled as part of Denmark. Shortly afterwards (*c.* 1539), King Christian III introduced the Reformation, and the Faroes become a Protestant diocese. The king immediately confiscated two-thirds of the Church land, including the priests' glebes, which left the priests in dire straits. Danish replaced Latin as the Church language, and the Catholic seminary was closed, but in 1547 a new Latin school was set up in Tórshavn; it lasted until 1804. Heine Jonsson, Magnus Heinason's father, was made the first dean of the Faroes, and the king confiscated the remaining third of the Church's property. The administration of the first lands to be confiscated by the Crown was given to the king's countryman, Thomas Koppen, on certain conditions. Koppen died in 1553, and trade became freer for a while, since the Faroese were now allowed to trade with Danish and Norwegian merchants but not with foreigners. However, the king decided, in 1556, to run the trade monopoly himself.

5　The Trade Monopoly (1556–1856)

Magnus Heinason and the Pirates

King Fredrik II of Norway (1559–88), who also happened to be King of Denmark, inherited the royal monopoly of trade with the Faroes but later handed it over to private individuals to run. In 1571 he even allowed the Faroese to trade at home and abroad, for a consideration, and among the first to take up his offer was Magnus Heinason (1545–89), the son of the first Faroese Lutheran dean.

Countless stories are told about how Magnus got the better of marauding pirates, but he was not a particularly good supplier of goods to the Faroes and was discharged in 1583, after many complaints, and so returned to Holland. He was later convicted of piracy and beheaded in 1589. Although praised by the Faroese, he was not much better than most other adventurers of his time.

After Magnus Heinason's downfall and until 1619, the monopoly was in the hands of various Copenhagen, Hamburg and Bergen merchants who had additional rights over the taxes from the Faroe islanders. In 1619 the Icelandic Company took over the monopolies of both Iceland and the Faroes until 1655, when the yearly royal income from the Faroes was 1,000 rigsdaler. The company was dissolved in 1662.

The Gabel Regime

The accession of the new king, Fredrik III, in 1648 heralded a change for the worse. Two of his ambassadors received the

Løgting's oath of allegiance to the king the following year, but in 1662 the king demanded, and gained, the acceptance of his being an absolute and despotic ruler. This development stood in stark contrast to the recent restoration of the monarchy in England; the results were completely opposite: one led to autocracy, the other resulted in democracy.

In 1655 began a half-century's misery under the so-called Gabel regime. Christoffer Gabel obtained the entire revenue from the Faroes against an annual rent of 1,000 rigsdaler – which, despite devaluation, was the same amount as it had been a century previously. In 1661 this privilege was extended to him and his son, Fredrik, for their lifetimes, without any increase in rent, and the following year they were granted the complete trade monopoly. This concession was readily given because the king was desperately short of ready money for the wars he was conducting.

Complaints about the incompetence and corruption of the Gabels' factors were investigated in 1672–3 by a Royal Commission but with little positive result. A local minister, Lucas Debes, had tried to alert the authorities in Copenhagen about the plight of the people but he was accused of inciting the people against local officials. He then wrote his famous book: *Færoæ et færoa reserata* (1673–4) – '*A description of the Faroes and its inhabitants*'. By a curious coincidence in that same year the Trade Monopoly's buildings, the *ting*-house and the fort's powder-magazine were all destroyed in an arson attack, which meant that the account books of the Gabels' agents were also, conveniently, not available for inspection over alleged fraud.

With the death of Gabel's heirs, the monopoly reverted back to the crown in 1709 and the Royal Trading Monopoly ruled the roost until 1856. This latter event ushered in an epoch that still dominates Faroese history and development, and whose influence is critical to an understanding of the Faroese situation today.

The Royal Trading Monopoly

Tithing (the 10 per cent) was the most important tax to be levied on everything and had four original components – for the bishop, the Church, the priest and the poor. After the

Reformation the king took the first quarter while the last quarter was abolished by Christian V's law. The items subject to the tithe were barley, wool, fish, butter, whales, seals and sea-birds, but the most important were wool and fish.

The royal bailiff and the current monopoly-holders had warehouses in Tórshavn on Tinganes where the taxes could be handed over and other goods purchased.

In the eighteenth century the exports had not changed substantially (how could they?) but the imports had altered, and additional demand arose for more luxury goods: tea, coffee, sugar, spices and tobacco, besides hemp, iron, lead, chalk, building-stone, tar, glass, nails, gunpowder and leather.

So the Royal Trading Monopoly (1709–1856) was never really a money-spinner but more of an unintentional subsidy since, for most of the time, it ran at a loss. However, some individual people made a lot out of their monopoly and their control over the thousand Faroese families in 1800, but other ways of trading were possible, like smuggling i.e. evading customs duties to the crown.

Niels Ryberg and Nólsoyar-Páll

A renowned Copenhagen merchant, Niels Ryberg, took advantage of this situation when the tax-haven and main British smuggling centre based on the Isle of Man closed down in 1765 after the Duke of Atholl sold up. Ryberg saw his chance and set up a transit-depot in Tórshavn in 1768 and staffed it with Manx, Irish and Scottish smugglers to take the contraband to Britain.

However, a legitimate trade was also present because in 1772 Ryberg was allowed to deal in the cod and herring trade from the Faroes. A factory was set up by the Danish firm of Rosenmeyer and Floor which taught the Faroese how to salt herring as well as how to make *klipfisk* – split, salted and dried cod. These products were then exported to the Baltic and Mediterranean, as they were to do later in the nineteenth century.

Rybergs Handel closed down in 1788 after the British drastically reduced the duty on tea. Nevertheless, the Faroese gained a great deal of experience in all sorts of crafts like coopering, carpentry, ship-building, fish-curing and office-work, besides being exposed to English-speakers. This influence was mainly felt in Tórshavn but it actually showed the Faroese that other economic possibilities existed in the outside world.

It was during this Ryberg period that the famous Faroese folk-hero Nólsoyar-Páll was born in 1766. He was bright and was encouraged in his learning by the king's bailiff, W. Hammershaimb. He had two brothers – Johannes, who learned much from Rosenmeyer of Rybergs Handel and later became a good farmer and a skilled boat-builder, and Jacob, who learned navigation and accountancy and then became the manager of the Royal Monopoly. Nólsoyar-Páll sailed in Ryberg's ships and also on the Monopoly's boats. He returned to the Faroes in 1800 and remarried after his first wife died, then became a large Crown-farmer in Klaksvík. His success in trading and farming led him to think about what improvements could be made to the economy, and he thought that free trade was the answer despite the general reluctance to accept these ideas.

Nólsoyar-Páll and a couple of farmers from Suðeroy tried to get a Treasury grant to build a boat, but this was refused and so they eventually brought the timbers from a wrecked boat to Tórshavn, where he and his brothers built a schooner in 1804. It was called *Royndin Friðar*: the beautiful experiment. He tried fishing without success and turned to trade but his attempts to sell Suðeroy coal and some sweaters met with opposition from the Monopoly who would not allow him to carry goods back to the Faroes. Nólsoyar-Páll satirized these officials in his famous 'Ballad of the Birds' where he likens them to birds of prey while he is only an oyster-catcher warning the smaller birds (i.e. the common people) of the others' evil intentions.

The outbreak of the Anglo-Danish war spelled disaster for Nólsoyar-Páll because when he sailed with a cargo of woollen sweaters to trade for grain he was captured by a British warship and taken to Sweden as a prize. His boat was wrecked. The British Admiralty compensated him by giving him another ship but after he left London in 1808 he was never heard of again. His achievements have been overestimated by the Faroese since he actually accomplished very little but he has remained a folk-hero, as a freedom-fighter.

The Danish governors

The Danish king's decision to join Napoleon led to his own ignominious defeat and the Treaty of Kiel in 1814 that separated Norway from Denmark but left the Faroes with a bankrupt Denmark. A Royal Commission of 1816 again found little support for the abolition of the monopoly in these circumstances. In that year the *Løgting* and the office of Lawman were abolished and the Faroes became a county of Denmark, under the provisional prefectship of Commandant Løbner who later became the first prefect or provincial governor in 1821.

This change in provincial government meant that the Faroes was drawn into the sphere of national responsibility and was no longer simply a faraway island. The job of prefect became part of a Civil Service career structure and not a quiet life in the backwoods. Fortunately it attracted some outstanding and enlightened officials after Løbner. First came the Tillisch brothers: Christian (1825–30) and Fredrik (1830–7). Christian was interested in education and tried to set up schools besides founding the provincial library in 1828 and the first hospital in Tórshavn in 1829. His brother, Fredrik, was concerned with economic improvements, such as introducing the plough and rationalizing the distribution of the whale-hunt, but his greatest triumph was the establishment of the Savings Bank (*Sparikassa*) in 1832.

The most popular and successful governor was Christian Pløyen (1837–48) who had previously been appointed the king's bailiff in 1830, which had given him time to learn the language and understand the problems of the economy. Indeed, it was he who composed the famous whale-hunting ballad that is still sung to this day. Pløyen believed that much was to be learned from their southern neighbours in Shetland and Orkney and he took some Faroese with him in 1839 to explore these possibilities. He was right. He introduced the use of Scottish seed-potatoes, the efficient Shetland peat-spade, the long-line method of fishing that used hundreds of hooks instead of the two hooks that the Faroese employed, besides getting men sent down to these Scottish islands to be trained in fish-curing.

Attempts had been made in the 1820s and 1830s to fish from

sloops but with disastrous results, as had Pløyen's suggestion to use decked boats. However, Nólsoyar-Páll's younger brother Jacob Nólsoe (1775–1869) had been placed in charge of the Royal Monopoly in 1831 and managed to turn round the finances from loss to profit through adventurous policies. This so impressed the next Royal Commission investigating the possible transition from monopoly to free trade that they recommended that Jacob should set up out-stations of the Monopoly, which he did at Tvøroyri (1836), Klaksvík (1838) and Vestmanna (1839). These branches were well placed and became the centres for further expansion after the abolition of the Monopoly in 1856. Other new incentives made by the Monopoly were to retrain the Faroese in the art of making *klipfisk* that they had forgotten, besides buying fresh fish for the first time. Pløyen welcomed all these improvements but he recommended to yet another Royal Commission in 1840 that free trade was better, to which they agreed and said the Monopoly should be ended in 1844 but constitutional reforms delayed its implementation until 1856.

II THE TRADITIONAL AND RECENT PAST (1848–1948)

Skopunarfjørður: Streymoy is to the right, Koltur is sticking up in the middle, Vágur is in the distance, Hestur is to the left.

Seascape

Grótvík: The weather is sometimes rough. This view is from Sandoy, Chapter 18.

The ferry: Norröna. This boat belonging to the Smyril Line operates between the Faroes and Scandinavia. See Appendix A. The photo shows her docked in Tórshavn.

Tindhólmur: This fairy-tale scene is taken from near Bøur on Vágur, Chapter 17.

Svínoy: The photo was taken from Viðareiði and shows the cliffs of Viðoy to the right and the island of Svínoy in the distance. See Chapter 16.

Elduvík: Here we see a typical *vik*, a small cove. What is of interest is the rocky silhouette of Kalsoy, behind. See Chapter 15.

Akraberg: The lighthouse is at the southernmost tip of the Faroes. See Chapter 19, Sumba.

Gjógv: This typical fissure gives its name to the village. See Chapter 15.

6 Farming

Until nearly the turn of the nineteenth century, farming was the chief economic activity and so, at that time, the Faroes could really be described as a collection of various farms gathered into villages, located on different islands. Then, all villages were compact and had access to the sea with near-lying boat-houses and a church near the shore, at the head of a bay or a fjord or on gently sloping ground under steep hills. The collection of houses that formed the village would be close to the cultivated infield (*bøur*), cut by drainage-ditches and cattle-roads into separate parcels of land; it would all be surrounded by the stone wall which separated the infield from the outfield (*hagi*). Beyond that boundary-wall lay the largest part of the village's land that stretched across the hills until it met the borders of neighbouring villages' outfields, where the sheep were kept. The eyes of the Faroese were firmly kept on any infringement of these land-boundaries with their associated rights.

Land tenure

A fascinating but complicated question is what exactly was the nature of the Faroese land-tenure system? On the one hand, it was responsible for the continuance of Faroese society for a millennium, yet it contained within itself the seeds of its own destruction and the marginalization of farming in our own century. This question is not simply a legal matter but one that lay at the very heart of Faroese society, since the possession of land determined the actual social structure.

In the Faroes, all land – the infield, the outfield, the fore-shore, the bird-cliffs, offshore-holms and islets – and every-thing pertaining to the land – peat, sand, seaweed, shellfish, fishing and whale-drives, floating timber, etc. – was owned by *somebody* – the Crown, private individuals or village com-munities. Nothing was unowned or unclaimed. Even today, the sea, the seabed, the mineral deposits (including oil) below the surface and the air-space above is claimed by someone or other.

Allocation of specific rights in land depended upon the system of assessment and the way of allocating land but the real origin of that system is unclear: the land was divided into units of a *mark* that was subdivided into sixteen *gylden* which itself was broken down into basic units of *skind* where one gylden equalled twenty skind, according to old Norwegian measurements. (The Faroese equivalents are *mørk*, *gyllin* and *skinn*, but the official land records were kept in Danish.) However, these units did not have any intrinsic value since the same area of land varied in value from place to place, so that one mark of land in one place could be worth seven times the same area in another place. This had little relation to the fertility of the soil or anything else like rights in bird fowling or whale catching. The real answer might, perhaps, lie in the value of the outfields, since the percentage that a person owned of the infield dictated the same percentage of his total outfield rights and its sheep population. Thus it might be that a person's original claim to so many sheep (as dictated by the *Sheep Letter*, Seyðabrævið, of 1298) determined the value of the infield acreage. This matter has not yet been resolved but it still meant that all the natural resources were divided up between the 'owners' of the village land.

Until 1899, the mark was used as the basis for land taxation and is still used to judge the wealth of the outfield; the largest villages on this scale are Hvalba (98.25 mark) and Sandur (97 mark) while the smallest are Norðskali on Eysturoy, and Norðtoftir on Borðoy, with only 4 marks each. The average village size on this scale is actually 10–50 marks.

Originally, the current villages were the sites of single farms that just expanded, yet claimed total rights to their territories, even if their legal rights were unclear. After the introduction of Christianity and the subsequent acknowledgement of the

Norwegian king by the local chiefs, they won back their respective rights on the basis of their tributes to the king. Their own tenants also obtained recognition if they paid their dues to their chiefs. At some point in time, an implicit relation between land-holders and the king gave them *udal* status, i.e. perpetual rights in the land, in return for dues to the king. These legal rights became even more complicated when the Catholic Church expropriated land as fines for misdemeanours, since the Church eventually acquired nearly half the available land by the time of the Reformation.

Around 1540, the Danish king, Christian III, accepted Protestantism and then confiscated two-thirds of the Catholic Church's property, which he lent out in perpetuity to farmers for an annual rent. These men then became Crown-farmers, on condition that their farms should never be divided and be inherited by only a single heir. This rule contradicted the older Norwegian *udal* law that property should be equally divided between all the heirs.

Thus a difference then arose between *udal*-holders and Crown-farmers regarding inheritance that was to have tremendous consequences over the next 400 years. The Crown-farmers started off with relatively large farms that continued to be the same size over the generations, whereas the *udal* farms were split up between the heirs after each generation, leading to a complete fragmentation of the original farms. To complicate matters, each heir had the right to an equal share of the good and the bad land, which led to every inheritor having ever smaller strips of good and bad land, *all over the infield*. The result was that the Crown-farmers became absolutely dominant as they had the largest shares of the infield and could dictate what should be done at the village council.

Laws of 1559 and 1673 further strengthened the position of the Crown-farmers, such that only their eldest sons could inherit the farm. An unexpected consequence of these laws was that the children of ministers received preference, if a Crown-farmer died intestate. The result was that it became extremely common for Danish ministers' sons to become farmers and marry into other Crown-farmers' families. Thus the ministers and Crown-farmers became closely inter-related and so emerged as the dominant élite in Faroese society.

Udal-farmers also tried to keep land in their families' possession by restricting the number of children they had and by
arranging skilful marriages, since it was common practice that
a man gave his bride a gift and for her parents to give a dowry
that was often in pieces of land. Such gifts were meant to be
equal in value and enabled the couple to set up a household.
This issue became very important between 1777 and 1846
since people could not be married by the minister if they did
not possess at least a half mark of land – the minimum it was
thought necessary to support a family. This ordinance was
actually directed against poor landless fishermen in order to
inhibit their getting married and producing children who
would then have to be supported by the communal, poor-relief
fund.

Some villages, like Skopun, had no infield at all of their own,
as they had been settled on the outfield of another village a
century or so ago. This type of land is called *trøð* and was
introduced by the government to provide the landless with a
plot on which they could grow potatoes. Such villages were
obviously poor, besides having no rights to the turbaries,
bird-cliffs or grazing, and so they did not all succeed.

Outfield land was the real key to the survival of a village and
so its use was therefore strictly controlled. The mountain part
of the outfield was for summer-grazing the sheep but could be
divided up into separate pastures, each with their own flocks
and shepherds. The lower outfield and the infield were for
winter pasturage, and the infield gates were then open between
25 October and 14 May. However in the summer growing
season the infield gates were kept locked and the walls had to
be constantly patrolled to prevent sheep jumping over them.
Outside the village wall itself, this part of the outfield was for
the summer-grazing of cattle and geese, besides being used for
getting peats, and turves for roofing.

Every spring a meeting of the landowners was called to
discuss the administration of the outfield, and the appointment
of shepherds and wall-inspectors. Voting was based on how
many *gylden* of infield an individual possessed, since his
proportion of the total infield carried with it the same ratio of
rights in the outfield, despite the latter's larger acreage. A
gylden allowed grazing rights for one and a half to three sheep,
depending on the quality of the outfield. Crown-farmers

always had a dominant say, since they owned most of the land.

Today, ninety-five settlements are reckoned up in terms of this ancient land-mark scale (*mark, gylden* and *skind*) but these settlements should not be confused with the present-day villages that are grouped into fifty local administrative units (*kommuner*). No fixed acreage existed for a mark of land because it all depended on the productivity of the soil. This 600-year-old system was the basis for taxation and tithes up to 1897. The land tax was based on the amount of land owned or leased and it was paid, like the tithes, in kind.

Splintering of *udal* land led to some villages having more than 1,000 separate parcels of land in the nineteenth century, which was quite uneconomic. Most countries in Northern Europe introduced enclosure acts to rationalize the land-holdings but this did not happen in the Faroes until 1928. Since then, a steady increase in the rationalization of the infields and outfields has taken place and the task is now almost complete. However, agriculture is now a minority occupation, and it is of little consequence that many of the once-precious infields have been built over for modern housing, roads and factories.

Agriculture

Barley and hay were the main crops grown in the Faroes together with a few root crops. Although potatoes were introduced in the eighteenth century they were not really accepted as a proper crop until the nineteenth century.

The current ribbed appearance of the sloping valley infields is due to the ancient mode of cultivating barley that went out of use at the turn of the century. The land was divided into stepped strips about 3 m wide and bounded by ditches on either side. The main implement used was the spade.

The only grain grown for human consumption was six-row barley which never ripened on the stalk but had to be specially dried. The ears of grain were first separated from the stalks by hand or by using a special tool and were dried either over the household fire or in a special house, *sornhús*. Villages often had several such drying houses for the use of different households.

Drying the grain actually took place on wooden platforms over a peat fire. The lighting of the fire was kept very secretive and generally performed by an old spinster, who was in complete charge. After the fire had died down and simply glowed, the young people were allowed in to enjoy the warmth, bake potatoes and listen to stories of the super-natural. It took twenty-four hours to dry a quantity of grain, after which the grain-drier called in a couple of women to help with threshing the grain on the tamped earthen floor. The winnowed grain was stored in bins in the lofts of the dwelling houses. Normally a quern was kept in the drying house and people were always excited to see how the harvest tasted.

The practice of barley cultivation ceased at the beginning of this century, as it was too labour-intensive and too many men were at the fishing for the tasks to be properly carried out.

HAYMAKING

Most of the cultivated fields today are devoted to grass and fed with artificial fertilizer. The grass is cut in August, after Ólavsøka on 29 July.

Hay is first spread on the ground to dry and then gathered into heaps before erecting small haycocks that were often weighted down with stones to prevent them from blowing away. Today some villages use fences to dry the hay upon. Eventually, the hay is brought back to the farm and made into a large haystack. Even today, two-legged haystacks may be seen, staggering towards the farmsteads, as men carry huge loads of hay home on their backs.

Until recently, special festivals were held in connection with bringing in the hay that was so vital for the sheep and cattle during the winter. All this activity demanded a large amount of labour but nowadays that is not available and so practices have changed. Some farmers use hay-cutters and small tractors in those villages whose infields have been rationalized and where the terrain permits. Very few farms today boast hay-stacks in their backyards – only silos.

PEAT GATHERING

Peat has always been the chief fuel in the Faroes and a well-defined set of rights is attached to lifting the peat that was normally linked to land ownership, though anyone who had the right to build a house could take as much peat as required. This led to complicated rules because if a house was divided then the peat banks were also divided. Peat could be dug only in certain defined places, which generally favoured the large landowners.

It was women's work to spread the peat out to dry after the men had dug it out. The dried peats were made into a large air-filled cube, ready for taking home in a wooden creel when required.

This century has seen a revolution in home heating: oil and electricity are practically universal. Only a few people nowadays bother to cut peat, although some still like it for old times' sake and its atmospheric smell.

CATTLE KEEPING

Cows have been kept in the Faroes ever since Viking days but those small cattle have been greatly improved over the centuries by the introduction of different races. Unlike sheep, cattle were kept inside during the winter in separate byres, or in an adjacent building to the dwelling-house, while poorer families even kept them in the house itself. Later on, cows were kept in a cellar beneath the house which provided both extra warmth and extra smells. This latter practice still continues but it has become quite rare since the day of the family cow has now passed.

Milking was traditionally a female responsibility, for it is only during this century that men began milking. Cows were milked twice a day, at about 8 a.m. and 8 p.m. was common. In the summer when the cows were in the outfield, they were milked by milk-maids who generally knitted as they went barefoot into the outfield, carrying with them several wooden milk-pails. Only in bad weather were they accompanied by a man, though a constant danger always remained from the bull. Once a year the milk-maids threw a party and, later, the young men joined in and they danced the night away.

This communal milking no longer takes place but it did continue right up until the 1960s. Cows were primarily kept for the household milk supply and also for their manure, but the shortage of fodder meant that scarcely 10 litres a day were obtained after calving. Although, after 1900, most domestic income came from fishing, the family cow and a potato patch were still absolutely essential to maintain the households of the poorer folk.

Today the Faroes are more or less self-sufficient in dairy produce but this is provided by professional dairy farmers who have large herds.

SHEEP FARMING

The Sheep Letter of 1298 laid down the basic rules for sheep farming and these are still followed today: sheep belong to the outfield and every village has one or more pastures in the outfield. Since the early Middle Ages two types of sheep-ownership have existed: joint and individual. In the first type a number of owners share the sheep and the labour involved, according to the amount of land they reach possess, but there is no question of individual ownership of any of the sheep. In the second type, individual owners can place so many sheep in the pasture as their land-ownership warrants. In the first instance, the profits and losses are shared but, in the second case, the individual alone suffers if anything goes wrong.

In the summer the shepherd drives the sheep as far up the mountainside as possible, bearing in mind their usual grazing areas. The sheep in each pasture are divided into different 'drives' that refer both to the number of sheep driven and to the territory where the sheep stay, for they are taught to keep to a limited area.

The outfield is the chief grazing area but the grassy edges of bird-cliffs can sometimes be used for a few sheep, while isolated stacks may be similarly employed. These areas are well manured by bird guano and the sheep can grow quite fat, and hence highly prized, but it involves problems in both taking the sheep there, and bringing them away again. Hoists and boats are sometimes required.

Sheep are gathered in the summer and autumn; the first drive is for shearing and the second is to choose the animals to be killed. Before that, in May, just after lambing, a round-up takes place when the lambs are marked with a special cut made on their ears. These marks are registered and vary from village to village so that identification is clearly established. In June the sheep are sheared with a penknife and the wool is taken to the village and shared out between the owners, though if individual ownership is the rule then the responsibility is on the owner. Michaelmas is the time to drive the sheep again, in order to slaughter the male lambs. If the terrain is inhospitable, the sheep may have to be carried home. In the evening, the sheep are divided up into those that are the shepherds' wages and the breeding-stock, while the rest have their feet bound and laid in rows to be divided between the owners. The best sheep were put at the head of the rows and the worst at the bottom. Owners drew lots, or took turns to select their sheep, but, if there were many owners, then it was necessary to divide the meat after the animals were killed, in order to ensure a just division between them.

Ideally, the sheep should be killed on the very evening after the division has taken place. Everything was used: the entrails were made into black pudding and stuffed tallow sausages, the carcase was cut up and hung to wind-dry in a special drying house (*hjallur*) and the skins tanned to be made into fleeces for sale.

The Faroese prize wind-dried mutton (*skerpikjøt*) above most other food and it is a source of pride to have produced a succulent leg of lamb to share with guests. Once upon a time '*Faroese wool was Faroese gold*', but today wool prices have dipped and the traditional knitwear is now machine-made from cheaper, imported Falkland wool. Shearing is hardly worthwhile and many sheep are now left to cast their wool naturally.

7 Fishing and Trading

Fishing and fishermen

The seas around the Faroes have always provided the people with their basic staple: fish. It is said that Faroese boys are born with an oar in their hands, and that a boatless man is a helpless man. Of course boats are necessary to travel in but the main use of Faroese boats has always been for fishing. Direct descendants of the Viking boats in form, their high prows are reminiscent of the dragon-headed warships that once sailed out of Norway.

Although fishing took place all year round, certain times were better than others. In the summer, small boats were used, but on about 1 November they were put in the boat-houses for the winter and, from then on, the eight-man boat was employed. Fish was caught for household needs all the year but, when cod started spawning on the Faroese banks, then cod fishing became more important. This fishing month, reckoned from the new moon at the end of January until the next new moon, gave fish that could be split and dried and sold as *stockfish*, besides yielding large amounts of liver and roe that were used at home. The next fishing period was the spring fishing that began about 12 March and lasted all April. Good fishing was possible between these two periods if the weather was fine but not otherwise. Later, when buyers first began to purchase fresh fish, especially after 1856, poorer fishermen could then earn enough during this period to buy goods from the shopkeepers.

A body of superstitious practices grew up around fishing. A keen interest was taken in knowing about the future of the boat. According to tradition, the boat-builder knew from the very first wood shaving he made, when starting to cut the wood, what the fate of the boat would be. So he often turned his head aside as he made his first stroke. If a special light was seen over the boat when it stood on the shore or in the boat-house, it spelled disaster. It was important whom you met on the way to fish – red-haired women were a bad omen. Certain birds, like crows, presaged disaster. A seal before a boat going out to fish meant an accident, but a seal after the boat was a good omen.

The boat should always be turned clockwise (with the sun), and was turned widdershins (against the sun) only when taking a body to a funeral. A boat should not bump into land once it had been launched. When baling out water it should always be from the starboard side, otherwise a bottle of schnapps had to be given to the rest of the crew in compensation for any resulting misfortune that could then be expected from the supernatural powers.

Men were always afraid of losing their fishing luck and they tried to keep it or renew it. A boat should never be seen empty and therefore one fish was always left in the boat. In relation to others, especially strangers, the danger of the evil eye and the evil tongue was always present. Bait was not borrowed from each other, unless special rules and behaviour were followed. Such beliefs remain part of the fisherman's world.

It was not always necessary to have to row out to catch fish, sometimes the fish came close to the shore and could be easily caught. The most important of these were saithe or coal-fish that spent the first two years of their life in vast shoals near the coast. They can be caught with a rod and hook by simply standing on the shore and casting for them, using whelks as bait or even nothing at all. An alternative method was to fish with a rod from a boat, when it was possible to go further out to catch larger saithe; this type of fishing was conducted between August and Christmas. Another method was to use nets that were hauled ashore with everyone lending a hand. These fish could be eaten fresh or dried, and their livers were reduced to train-oil, that could be sold or used for lighting.

Merchants

Midway through the nineteenth century the role of the merchant took on an added importance, with the introduction of free trade. It has to be remembered that the Royal Monopoly was not an ordinary commercial undertaking, for it was not so much a profit-making enterprise as a welfare office. The Monopoly had already set up out-stations at important fishing villages in order to buy in produce: hose, fish, oil, etc., and villagers no longer had to row long distances to the warehouse in Tórshavn in order to obtain essential supplies. Furthermore, the prices were fixed in 1691 and hardly changed much until 1801 when they began to reflect their market price. Thus people felt a certain security, especially as the Monopoly had to purchase whatever they had to offer. Things began to change as free trade loomed nearer.

Several attempts had been made since the 1820s to conduct fishing from decked boats but most of them proved financially unrewarding. Two main reasons explain this failure: the low prices paid for fish by the Monopoly, and the lack of experienced fishermen. Despite State loans, these enterprises also failed because the wages were so low that only the landless poor were interested.

Free trade

The introduction of free trade meant that anyone over twenty-five years of age could apply to obtain a licence to trade. In the first year alone, some 105 people had obtained permission to trade, mainly in Tórshavn. Within three years, most villages had a shop. The Monopoly's buildings were sold off. It is important to note that all these buyers and traders were foreigners – not Faroese.

It was not long before the Faroese themselves also entered commercial activities. The larger merchants then divided the Faroes between them, but in some villages, rival shopkeepers, belonging to different firms, competed with each other. Many of these firms are still there today.

These merchants bound the Faroes into a single trading entity by rationalizing the distribution of goods to the villages; their dependent shopkeepers also helped the merchants with collecting fish and other goods for eventual sale abroad. As middlemen between the ordinary people and the merchants, some shopkeepers abused their position through the sale of alcohol and offering fishermen and petty farmers drinks on credit. A lot of land was signed away by indebted persons who could not pay these bills. This alcohol abuse led to many protests and eventually to a referendum in 1907 that banned the sale of alcohol in the Faroes – a prohibition that is still in force.

The rise of the merchants to a dominating position in the Faroes was not because more home agricultural produce was for sale – almost the opposite. The population had grown from 5,000 in 1800 to 8,000 in 1850 yet the area of cultivated land was unchanged as was the total permitted sheep population. Thus people had to depend on imported grain sold by the merchants. What made all the difference was the rise of fishing activities.

Salted fish was traditionally not very common because salt was difficult to come by and it was not until free trade that this type of fish became an export item. What made the Faroese fishing really take off was the production of *klipfisk*, but this did not occur until the end of the Monopoly period.

Klipfisk and the export trade

Klipfisk is cod that has been split, dried and salted: its name derives from being dried on rocks (*klippe*). In the seventeenth century the biggest production of *klipfisk* was in Møre, Norway. It was exported to the Mediterranean, especially to Spain where it was called *bacalao*. This product was also exported from Shetland, but there was little contact between the Faroes and Shetland until Pløyen's day. The production of *klipfisk* was actually introduced into the Faroes during Ryberg's trading enterprise from 1768 to 1788, after which it was forgotten until Pløyen reintroduced it in 1835; but the prices were still not right. Only after 1841 was the production of *klipfisk* taken up again. All this fish was caught from open boats around the Faroes; what had revolutionized the production was the use of the long-line that Pløyen had introduced from Shetland. Yet another revolution was to take place in 1872 that raised the catch 60 years on, in 1922, to 5,000 tons of *klipfisk* and 6,000 tons of salt fish. This revolution was due to the successful use of sloops for fishing.

By the mid-nineteenth century, the British fishing fleet had gone over to steam trawling and was going further afield to Iceland and Norway in search of cod; thus a number of sailing sloops were going cheap in Britain. The Faroese fishing revolution came when three brothers from Tórshavn, called Haraldsen, went to Scarborough and bought the 38-ton sloop *The Fox* and brought it home in 1872. They immediately set sail in the summer for Iceland and fished for cod, from small boats as usual, that brought their catch back to their mother vessel. Next spring they fished the Faroese banks and again they were successful. This encouraged others to buy these old sloops and within a few years there were a dozen such boats. Success bred success, and by the turn of the century eighty sloops were fishing from the Faroes and the pattern of sloop fishing was thus established, with spring and autumn Iceland fishing that dominated Faroese life until the Second World War, when there were 162 sloops.

Until 1930, these sloops were powered only by sails but after that auxiliary motors were installed. The crew numbered between twelve and twenty men. They set sail for the south coast of Iceland at the beginning of March and returned home in May for a fortnight's break. Then, off they went to east and north Iceland until the beginning of October. The crew just stood by the gunwale and each man used a fishing line with two hooks and a sinker to catch the cod. The fish were cleansed and salted onboard. For the rest of the year they fished around the Faroes in small boats while the sloops were laid up. Most of the salted fish was later dried to make *klipfisk*.

The total population also grew during the sloop period: from 10,000 in 1872 to 29,000 in 1945. At the beginning of this period half the people gained their livelihood from the land while only a quarter derived it from fishing. By the end of this period only 5 per cent were fully engaged in agriculture while half were employed in fishing activities.

The economic infrastructure

For this economic revolution to occur, it needed entrepreneurs: merchants, shopkeepers, shipowners and skippers who would take a chance. This development was first encouraged by the creation of the Faroese Savings Bank, *Sparikassa*, set up by governor Tillisch in 1833. In 1906 a new bank – *Føroya Banki* (The Faroese bank) – was set up in order to promote more economic progress. By the outbreak of the Second World War, the total deposits were only 9 million kr. The war-time profits (1940–5) of running fish to Britain had swollen the net assets in the banks to 36 million kr. by 1945. In 1950, the end of this period being considered, the banks had deposits of 60 million kr. This vast expansion in savings disguises all the other money that had been invested in material possessions – ships, houses, goods, etc. Actually the standard of living in the Faroes in 1950 was still little better than in Britain at the turn of the century.

The development of the fishing industry

Before *The Fox*'s success in cod fishing off Iceland, most fishing was confined to local rowing-boats around the Faroes. Some 1,000–1,500 such boats went out catching local cod around the Faroes.

In 1936 many Faroese companies went bankrupt because of foreign wars and so the Danish government set up a special fund to help those affected. In the same year, an export monopoly was set up to oversee the export of *klipfisk* and salt fish; it was called the Faroese Fishexport. This cooperative found other new markets and laid the basis for a post-war organization for exporting fish: *Føroyar Fiskasøla* (Faroe Seafood).

In the very early days several men joined together to purchase a ship, but they gradually became dependent on a merchant who bought their catches. The commonest export was *klipfisk* and this was often processed by women under the supervision of the merchant himself. The catches of cod were washed, cleaned and laid out to dry on rocks or large stony areas. Care had to be taken not to let the fish spoil, if it rained. It was not until the 1930s and 1940s that the drying process was mechanized and carried out inside buildings heated with warm air. The *klipfisk* industry provided women with an income that had not been possible earlier on. In the larger villages on Suðuroy, where sloop fishing was largely based to begin with, the shortage of local female labour led to girls from other villages migrating there to work in the high season.

Merchants not only took over the fitting-out of the boats,

they also ran and owned the boats. Some boats were individually owned by various merchants, although partnerships were made between merchants and skippers. The ordinary fishermen rarely had shares in the boat. In 1909 the shipowners formed a federation to regulate conditions and prices, and in 1911 the fishermen themselves also became unionized. Normally the crew received a third of the proceeds while the skipper got 10 per cent and the mate 1 per cent; the cook received a monthly wage. Each fisherman's share was worked out on the basis of his contribution to the total catch.

With the introduction of auxiliary motors and the purchase of larger, old sloops, the Faroese were now able to sail further afield to Greenland. Still using hand-held fishing-lines, the Faroese sloops off Greenland could get double their usual catch off Iceland. In the depression in the 30s, and with shrinking catches elsewhere because of failing fish-stocks on the Faroe banks and off Iceland due to intensive trawling by other nations, this opportunity was a godsend but they had to battle for their rights every single year.

The Faroes were occupied by the British during the Second World War after Denmark's surrender to the Germans in April 1940. The Icelandic and Greenland fishing continued that year and the catch was made into *klipfisk* and salt fish as usual, but the market was restricted. What Britain needed was fresh fish but the Icelanders refused to sail to Britain without air-protection and so it fell to the Faroese to ferry fresh fish from Iceland to Scotland. This did not, of course, need large crews and unemployment occurred, but this was recompensed by the high prices paid for this fish. The Faroese supplied Britain with about 20 per cent of all the fish eaten there during the war. These exports were worth nearly 40 million kr. annually, while the sterling balances in Britain rose to nearly £3 million pounds sterling by the end of the war. For this enormous boost to the economy, a price had to be paid: twenty-five boats were lost to enemy attack and 132 fishermen killed. With the end of the war the Faroese looked forward to continued prosperity from fishing but with a modernized fishing fleet bought with their newfound riches. Every village wanted to have its own trawler and new ship-owning firms started up, with assistance from the Løgting's Industrial Loan Fund to run these boats. It went well for a couple of years but then the bubble burst in 1950.

8 Whaling

Two types of whaling have been practised in the Faroes: the traditional pilot whale hunt and the large whale hunt.

We will begin by looking at the more recent form. As large whales like the blue, humpback and sperm whales became scarcer off the coast of Norway, Norwegian whalers extended their search to Iceland in 1883. Then in 1894 a Norwegian lighthouse-keeper started up at Gjánoyri in the Faroes to process and sell whale meat. Several other stations were built at Hvannasund, Funningsfjørður, við Air, Kollafjørður and Lopra. To begin with 17 whaling boats operated from here. The largest number of whales captured per boat was in 1900 when 66 whales per boat were caught. A record catch was made in 1909 when 773 whales were caught that year but thereafter it went into decline. Between 1911–14 the catch had dropped to 20 whales per boat. At the beginning of the Second World War, only two stations remained: við Air on Streymoy and Lopra in Suðuroy. The numbers of whalers rose to 7 and there was a record catch of 72 whales per boat in 1950. Thereafter, the number of catches decreased and these two stations closed down in 1959. A private company restarted whale catching in 1962 but only 19 whales were caught annually and the við Air station closed in 1966. Whale hunting was thus a brief interlude at the turn of the century since the whales were not that numerous.

The main types of large whale caught were fin whale, sei whale, blue whale and sperm whale. A small whale, the bottle-nosed, that grows only to about 7.5 m long was frequently caught in September by the people, at the appropriately named village of Hvalba, in Suðuroy. Only a handful are caught by driving them towards the shore and then hauling them ashore using a grapnel.

The most important indigenous whale hunt is for the pilot whale, blackfish or caaing whale (*grind* in Faroese), a small-toothed whale. Males can measure up to 8 m long while females are only half that size. They are immensely gregarious and swim in schools varying in size from twenty to 2000 strong. They can be caught all the year round but particularly in the summer months. Statistics have been kept on pilot whale catches ever since 1584 and these show great variations over time; whale-less years meant great hardship, as the blubber and meat formed an essential part of the Faroese diet, then as now. However, the economic importance of this whale catch has less significance nowadays, though its emotional significance has not changed. Up to this century, caaing whales were also caught in Orkney and Shetland. Indeed, their very name comes from Shetland: *caaing* refers to driving sheep into a fold, just as the whales are driven into a bay.

The one single thing that used to galvanize all Faroese men into furious purposeful activity was the knowledge that a school of pilot whales had been sighted. When a school of whales was spotted from on land one shouted out '*grindaboð*' – a message that there were whales about. This cry was repeated by all who heard it and so the message spread. It was a punishable offence to raise a false alarm. Every village was responsible for passing on the news to the next one: one ran or rowed to the next village, spread out a sheet, cut the turf in a certain way or lit a bonfire. It was necessary to gather as many boats together as possible for the whale drive, since not enough boats were available in any single village.

If the school was spotted from a boat then a piece of clothing was hauled up from the mast. This is the traditional signal that everyone knows, though today it merely indicates who found the school. Nowadays the message is sent by telephone on land and by radio if at sea. The Faroese national radio used to broadcast if pilot whales had been seen and kept people up-to-date about where the whales were heading. Today, only the fact that a hunt has already taken place is announced.

Before Home Rule in 1948, the highest authority at a whale drive was the governor and he was supposed to lead all the Faroese drives. In practice, it was the local leader of the hunt and the sheriff who directed the drive to one of the authorized whaling bays, of which there were a dozen main bays. Each bay had four appointed leaders, who were formerly appointed by the governor, but after 1857 they were chosen by the village assembly for five years at a time.

When the '*grindaboð*' message is heard then men would rush home to get their whaling tools and down to their boats. Before the introduction of engines one had to row or sail to where the school had been sighted. The boats formed up behind the school of whales and drove them like a sheep towards one of the whaling bays. This was done by either throwing loose seashore pebbles into the water behind the whales or using a special rounded stone, painted white and tied to a line that could be used time and again. Even echo-finders have been found useful to drive the whales. The whales keep close together, but only about a fifth of them can be seen at any one time, when they come up to breathe. In the driving it is necessary to take into account the currents and wind direction. When the school gets close to two rival whaling bays then competition can occur to drive them into one bay rather than another. Sometimes unfair means may be used to out-manoeuvre a rival, like dropping herring dye in front of whales – this causes a blue curtain to appear and causes the whales to veer away. The ideal whaling bay is at the head of a fjord with a sloping beach. Once penned in between the sides of the fjord, the chasing boats form a solid line from shore to shore and splash away to keep the school moving forward.

The whale hunt proper begins on a given signal, either when one passes a certain geographical point or when the leader of the drive indicates it. Then the last whale astern in the school is stuck with a whale spear. It bounds forward and is followed by the rest of the school. If the beach is gradually sloping then the whales beach themselves, carried forward by the waves they themselves have created. Awaiting them are a crowd of men armed with sharp sheath knives, ready to cut the whales' necks. The blubber is slit open a handsbreadth behind the breathing-hole and the spinal column is severed between the head and the first vertebra, killing the whale instantly. If the whales do not beach themselves then the men wade out and secure them with an iron hook while their necks are being cut. However, if the whales are cornered, but not beached, then they are attacked with whale spears from the boats that makes a quick kill more difficult. Meanwhile, the seas become red with the blood of the whales which acts as a trap for any whale that has escaped under the line of boats, because they seek their way back to their dead fellows.

When all the whales are dead, they are dragged ashore and lined up in rows above the tidal-limit. Now the sheriff takes over the direction of sharing out the whales. He sets a guard over the whales so that nobody steals any of the meat, although anyone can take the liver. He also sends off people to recover any sunken whales. Then, together with his assistants, he numbers and evaluates the whales. Each whale receives a running number and an evaluation number. The running number is cut into the whale's head and the evaluation number is written in Roman numerals on one of the side-fins. Whales are evaluated in *gyllin* and *skinn* where 20 skinn are reckoned to a gyllin. A special ruler is used and the size is measured from the eye to the anus. Although a whale measuring 3.15 m is valued at 1 gyllin, they are most unusual. One skinn corresponds to roughly 50 kg of meat and 25 kg of blubber.

Many changes to the distribution of the catch have been made over time. Today, the procedure is to separate out some of the catch to cover certain outgoings. Firstly, the largest whale goes to the boat that first spotted the school of whales. Secondly, the sheriff and his helpers receive a percentage of the total catch. Some goes to the men who have participated in the hunt, while some are sold by auction to pay for any damage to boats that might have occurred during the hunt. The rest of the catch is divided up, according to in which bay the hunt ended.

Until 1934 a quarter of the whole catch was divided between the landowners in the whaling bay who had the rights to the shore. At one time the landowners could claim half the catch. After 1934 these land-rights were abolished and the catch was divided between members of a whaling district. The Faroes is divided into nine whaling districts, based on the whaling bays. Every member of a district is entitled to a share of the catch, except for Tórshavn which is too large and therefore too complicated to work out the shares. Each whaling district is divided into smaller units based on villages; larger villages may themselves be divided into units that may have names. Everyone in a village is a member of one of these units – the newborn, new householders and incomers can be registered with the sheriff. Each unit has a leader who sees to it that the catch is collected and divided up.

Each whaling district is divided up into 'boats' – roughly fifty persons – and hence every district is reckoned in terms of so many boats. Even people from other villages who register with the sheriff within a certain period can receive a share. However, the recent good communications mean that hundreds of spectators can turn up and claim a share without having participated in the hunt – a cause of resentment.

Whilst the sheriff is reckoning out who gets what, the hunters and others dance the whale dance. The purpose originally was to warm the wet hunters; today it is just a celebration.

Recently, noticeable changes in conducting the hunt have been made because of intense lobbying by external conservationist groups like *Greenpeace*. It is now all very low-key and no details are broadcast about where a hunt is taking place. Bad publicity abroad, caused by sensationalist, gory television broadcasts in Europe, have embarrassed both the Faroese and Danish governments. Steps have been taken to reduce unnecessary suffering and so spears and grapnels have been banned. The Faroese were genuinely surprised by these hostile attitudes expressed by foreigners to their traditional hunt, particularly because pilot whales are not an endangered species. *Greenpeace* has admitted as much and has withdrawn its objections to the hunt, but other groups still oppose it on principle. Tourists are now requested not to take photographs as it might damage the image of the Faroes.

At one time, the Faroese also hunted seals like many other people in the North Atlantic. It was of importance to certain villages where seals lived. Two types of seal lived in the Faroes: the grey seal and the common seal. The former lived in sea grottoes, in the rocky cliffsides, while the latter lived on skerries. The grey seal pups were hunted in the autumn by being clubbed to death in their grottoes. The common seal was tamer and this led to its eventual extinction. The catch belonged to the landowners and they received the greater share. The meat and blubber were dried or salted while the skins were made into shoes.

It should be remembered that on these rocky islands all animal life had to be exploited if the people were to survive. This condition lasted up to this century when fishing enabled the Faroese to import food they could not supply themselves.

9   Fowling

An important source of fresh meat, always in short supply, was obtained by catching birds. Millions of sea-birds flock to the Faroes and the most commonly caught are the puffin and the guillemot. During this century the fulmar has also become important since it may be caught in the winter, whereas the other birds are normally taken in the summer. Egg-collecting was also important.

The main fowling cliffs lie on the western and northern coasts of the islands, where they often rise precipitously out of the sea. These near-vertical cliffs have alternate layers of basalt and tuff, providing a series of ledges up the rockface that suit the different breeding requirements of different species of birds that nest there, besides giving the fowler a foothold in his difficult task. At the bottom of the cliffs, fallen rocks also provide shelter for some birds.

The numbers of birds taken annually is difficult to estimate because no official statistics have been kept, but it is likely to have been at least 300,000 birds every year. This seemed to be true even in 1961, thirty-six years after the main bird-catching technique of *fygling* had been discontinued. Likewise, the number of eggs collected could have been about 100,000 annually and the main method – *raening* – was still continuing in 1974. Besides providing food, the birds' feathers were sold to the Monopoly; in 1850 some 18,000 lb were delivered and this represents the feathers of some 270,000 birds, not counting those used in the home.

The most valuable bird to be caught is the puffin. It is said that in a good year almost half a million puffins were caught in the islands, but the numbers caught are much reduced nowadays, as interest has declined. Puffins generally nest at the top of the bird-cliffs and they live in holes they dig in the turf. They lay one egg in May. A certain type of fowling begins straightaway when the birds are dragged from their holes and their necks are broken. It is possible to use bare hands, but if the hole is too long, then a special puffin hook is employed. This is a 60-cm long stick with a hook at the end. Should the nest be in a long tunnel, then a shaft is sunk into the turf to reach the bird and its egg. This shaft is carefully filled in later, so that the tunnel can be used by another pair. This method of fowling takes place for a few days so that it does not upset the strength of the colony. Sometimes the fowler has to use a rope to reach the place where the puffins nest, but this is a messy task and is only resorted to if there are no alternatives. The catch belongs to the land-owners as only they are allowed to hunt on the land.

2 July is the beginning of the fowling period for puffins and guillemots, using a fowling pole. This instrument is 3-m long with a triangular net at the end. It is used in special places on the fowling cliffs called 'seats'. A 'seat' is basically a flat stone to sit on that is shielded around with rocks and turf. The position of these seats are dictated by the nesting places. Nesting puffins fly in a straight line direct to their nests while the young birds fly in circles. The puffins who are bringing back fish for their young (*sildberin*; herring bearers), are not caught, only the young ones are taken. It is important that the seat is placed so that the flying circle of the birds is within the compass of the fowling pole. The circle depends on the wind direction as the birds always fly into the wind when they come close to land. The pole is held in both hands and is laid on the ground while waiting. As soon as a bird approaches, the pole is swung up and it catches the bird in the net from behind. Sometimes decoys are set up to attract the birds' attention.

A fowling pole can also be used from a boat, especially when catching guillemots. Rowing along the base of the fowling cliffs, one man keeps his pole aft and another one astern. If the birds are not startled then the oars are splashed, but the catch was never very great, even if it was free. Another way was to catch those guillemots that sat on low rocks by the water's edge. Several people took part and they rowed towards the rocks and dropped their fowling nets over the sitting birds, but as the poles would have touched the rocks, they had infringed the shore-rights and so the catch had to be shared with the land-owners. One way to avoid this pay-out was to use an Icelandic method in which a noose was attached to the end of a long pole. The loop was placed around the guillemot's neck, as it stood on the rocks, and lifted off; but, naturally, this could be done only one at a time. This idea came in at the end of the nineteenth century, but a more recent Icelandic method is the floating snare. Here, rows of snares are set up on a board together with a decoy and floated in the water. When the guillemots land on the board to rest, they are ensnared. A half-dozen such boards are cast out on the tides and visited from time to time. It is quite common nowadays just to go out in a boat and simply shoot the birds.

Under certain conditions puffins and guillemots are cast up by the wind over the top of the bird-cliffs and then fall to the ground. They are chased and hit with a stick. Normally the catch is not large but if the wind is southerly, hundreds might be caught in this fashion. When young guillemots leave their ledges they gather together in large swimming flocks since they cannot then fly. They can be herded by several boats and driven into an inlet where they can be dispatched with a stone tied to the end of a pole.

Normally, puffins and guillemots are hunted in the summer before they fly away out to sea. The fulmar is also caught with the fowling rod but since it is now practically a resident they are generally caught in the winter. Like young guillemots, the young fulmars are unable to fly. They leave their nests in the summer and gather on the water. The catching of young fulmars was forbidden in 1936 after it was discovered that people were being infected with psittacosis. Women, who were mainly responsible for plucking these birds, fell ill with what was called the 'September sickness'. Adult birds do not suffer from this disease and so they are still caught with the fowling pole.

The most dangerous form of fowling is *fygling* when fowlers were let down the steep sides of the bird-cliffs. It has been practised for centuries but ceased in 1925, for practical and economic reasons. Guillemots were caught with a fowling pole that was shorter than usual and had a larger net, but to reach their nesting places it was necessary to be lowered by rope 100 m or so down the cliffs. In some places, like Skúvoy, broad ledges were to be found half-way down the cliffs on which the fowlers could camp and also let themselves down even further.

Fygling demanded a well-organized team to be successful. Firstly, two men went down the cliffs and directed operations. They often worked in conjunction with a retired fowler who knew the ropes and rocks. In Skúvoy they used three ropes to descend the cliffs. Each rope was 146 m long and 9 cm thick, and took six men to carry it. At the edge of the cliff, two stout pegs were driven into the ground and the ropes were wound around them and acted as a brake. One reliable man saw to the rope while the first fowler made his descent. Another man kept in contact with the fowler and gave instructions to the man by the pegs, so that he could regulate the speed of descent. Generally, a piece of wood was placed at the cliff edge over which the rope travelled so that it would not cut into the ground.

It was important that the first man down was bound to the rope in the right way. He sat in a kind of rope seat that was fastened around his waist, legs and shoulders so that he did not tip over. He carried with him a fowling pole or an egg-ladle pole that had an iron tip that he used to thrust against the cliff to prevent him from spinning. Always a danger were falling rocks, for even the smallest stone could be a hazard, and so the first man down tried to dislodge any loose rocks. As the fowler went lower it became more difficult to make out his words and so an extra signal line was used. The simplest type was a cord on which he pulled, according to an agreed code. Telephones were also tried but the wires often broke. Even walkie-talkies have been used more recently in egg-collecting.

In Skúvoy, some dozen men were lowered down onto a broad shelf and two fowlers were then lowered further down to the guillemots. It would take four or five men to haul up the fowler again. Fowling lasted some three days and the fowlers took provisions with them. Occasionally it was necessary for a fowler to swing himself in under an overhanging cliff to reach the birds. This needed experience because it was all too easy to spin round and lose control. When possible, the fowler could be lowered into a waiting boat.

A three-day stint could net some 10,000 guillemots. These

were either lowered into a boat or hoisted up to the top. In the latter case, it could take the whole village's population to lift up the catch and the men. The division of the catch was made after fixed rules – the main fowler receiving seven times as much as the others, while a third went to the landowners.

Ræning or egg-collecting was mainly practised on Skúvoy and continued until 1974. The procedure is the same as *fygling*. The fowler has his egg pole, to reach eggs out of normal reach, and a tanned sheepskin bag that could hold 200 eggs. A few days' work could net 20,000 eggs. The principles of division were the same as for *fygling*.

Besides climbing down cliffs, it was also possible to climb up the cliffs and stacks. As a help, iron bolts and rings were fixed to the rocks to help the fowler haul himself both up and down.

A special type of fowling took place on Mykines where the only gannetry exists in the Faroes. Adult gannets were caught in the spring and the young in the autumn. The catching of adults took place at night. The fowlers were let down nearly 100 m or so to five different nesting places. The fowlers then cast themselves over the sleeping gannets and tried to catch as many as possible. The birds were killed quietly so as not awaken the other gannets. On pulling their signal line the fowlers were hoisted back up again. The catch was collected at dawn; either it was thrown down to waiting boats or was pulled up to the top of the cliffs. This method had fallen into disuse after the recent depopulation of the island.

As has been mentioned earlier, fowling has become rarer in recent years and with it the knowledge of the cliffs and the nesting places. The ledges and 'seats' often have special names and were inheritable. Today, fowling joins other traditional activities as mainly a thing of the past.

10   Culture and Customs

The Church

The mainstay of any culture is religion, and in the case of the Faroes today it has been Lutheran Christianity that came with the Reformation. There were churches in most villages and whilst the oldest still existing are only 150 years old, they are some of the most attractive buildings in the Faroes. Only a dozen of these small buildings survive. The Lutheran doctrine was implanted by the reading of Jesper Brochmand's teachings that were read in Danish by the deacon, when the minister did not conduct the service.

The role of the ministers was very important since only seven of them were available to conduct services in thirty-nine parishes, which meant they could get round only every six weeks or so. The parishioners were conservative and used Kingo's psalms ever since the middle of the nineteenth century and distrusted modern innovations. Communion was held only a few times a year and then the people were reminded by the church bells on the Friday beforehand, so they could air their best clothes for the service.

All the old churches had a rectangular plan with a weapon house, nave and choir. The walls were of upright planks and the roof was made with the traditional birch lining for a turf roof. The inside was unpainted and of scrubbed pine while the only decoration was on the side of the pews and the rood screen. Votive offerings were usually brass candelabra and model boats, besides painted altar pieces. Since the mid-nineteenth century other materials like stone and concrete have been used for building, but they generally followed the old plan and have corrugated iron or slate roofs. Only the most recent churches have completely broken away from tradition.

The Lutheran Church no longer has a monopoly of faith, for some 10 per cent of the population are now members of the Plymouth Brethren. The first missionary, W. B. Sloan, came to the Faroes from Scotland in 1865 and found many followers among fishermen. Thirty-four meeting houses are to be found around the islands, but the largest one is 'Ebenezer', in the middle of Tórshavn.

Song and dance

In the Faroes, singing and dancing are tightly related. No traditional musical instrument is employed other than the human voice and this goes hand-in-hand, so to speak, with the stomping rhythm of human feet, in the medieval chain ring-dance, for which the Faroes are so renowned. It was only in this century that the so-called English dance, i.e. modern dancing, has been taken up.

Ring-dancing was widespread throughout Europe in the Middle Ages but is preserved only here, while the songs or ballads (*kvæði*) are still medieval in their reference. Dancing was the most popular form of entertainment at all festive gatherings in the Faroes, and the dance period during the winter lasted from Boxing Day to the beginning of Lent and was resumed again only after Easter.

Men and women participate in the dance, in no particular order, by joining hands and forming a circle, waiting for the leader of the song to begin. The steps keep in time with the beat of the ballad. Everyone takes two steps to the left and then one to the right, so that you move gradually in a clockwise direction. The song-leader needs a strong and clear voice to guide the company; he begins each verse while the others join in the refrain, for it is insulting to accompany the leader's singing of the main stanzas. These ballads were often regarded as a form of personal property that belonged to particular leaders. It was not done to sing the same ballad again during the same winter, and it meant that leaders must have a large repertoire to keep the dance going.

The Faroese ballads (*kvæði*) were collected together in the nineteenth century and published as *Corpus Carminum Færoensium* (1951–68) in sixteen volumes: it has 234 ballads totalling 70,000 verses which works out, on average, to 300 verses per ballad! The themes come from the European chanson repertoire and include such items as the song cycle on Sigurd Fafnesbane from the Scandinavian version of the *Nibelungenlied,* as well as one on Charlemagne. Many ballads are set in an Icelandic or Norwegian milieux, while after the Reformation a number of shorter, heroic Danish ballads with a livelier tune were introduced, as well as popular broadsheet ballads.

A special type of satirical song (*táttur*) was composed to attack people who had broken the norms and which exposed them to ridicule. The best known of these satires were composed by Nólsoyar-Páll against the Danish officials of the early nineteenth century, while the Danish administrator Pløyen wrote the ever-popular ballad *Grindevisen* that has been sung after every whale hunt for the last 150 years.

These songs and dances took place on special dance evenings or at weddings, but the learning and rehearsal of the ballads took place in the evenings at the so-called '*kvøldseta*' in the 'smoky-room' (*roykstova*), when men span and women carded, while sagas and stories were related to pass the time. The dances were in fact held in a pre-booked smoky-room for they were held in various homes in rotation. However, at the end of the nineteenth century young people began to build special dance-halls where they could escape the sharp eyes of their elders in the smoky-room. It was necessary that such buildings had a springy floor that 'gave' with the regular stamp of feet, so that the people and building swayed simultaneously. It was common that the dance-hall was opened every Sunday evening during the dancing season where, at 6 p.m., young children could learn the steps, songs and ballads under the supervision of a few adults. At 8 p.m. the youths began to dance to easy songs. Later, the adults arrived and they danced properly until midnight, but on festival days they danced the night away.

At the end of the nineteenth century various changes altered this picture: increasing wealth among fishermen led to the overindulgent use of schnapps at the dance halls, while at the same time, a revivalist movement considered both alcohol and dancing to be most un-Christian. The missionaries succeeded in branding the Faroese ring-dance as a very sinful activity, and as late as 1977, when the Faroese Post Office issued a Christmas stamp depicting a ring-dance, these ministers advised their flocks to boycott this stamp! *Sic transit*. . . .

The traditional Faroese dance had already disappeared from its original milieu by the turn of the century, but the current nationalist revival sparked new life into old things, like the ballads and dance. Since then interest has waxed and waned but several places like Sumba, Sørvág and Gøta have formed clubs to preserve the Faroese dance and ballads. Otherwise, most dance places have discos but they do, occasionally and spontaneously, suddenly break into a Faroese ring-dance for a change.

Work holidays

The yearly agricultural round produced certain times for celebration, and the most important feast after the haymaking celebrations in the autumn was a general thank you party for all who had helped on the farm, the sheep drive, the ditching, wall repairs, and sheep-fold building. This feast, hosted by the farmer, usually took place after the sheep had been slaughtered, when the carcass could be sold for schnapps.

Another feast that used to be held was for the boat crews who were responsible for manning the village boat that was employed for fishing, as well as for transporting the minister and other officials. This took place between Christmas and New Year on a Sunday when, after church, the members assembled at the house of the captain, where they received lunch and supper. Afterwards they played cards and danced, at which women could join in. A minister, who had a boat, also had such parties, but the growing abuse of alcohol caused them to desist from such celebrations.

If somebody built a house, a party was held between Christmas and New Year for all those who had helped. The women came when it was ready to begin dancing. When the roof was raised, a small party with schnapps was given and the people then danced to stamp the earthen floor flat.

An all-female feast was held for the milk-maids and was especially prominent between 1900–30, but we do not know if it goes back further in time. The custom varied from village to village: some had an open-air feast in the late summer where everybody brought their own refreshments and where they danced into the night. Other villages held their feast inside, during the winter, when those households who had a milk-maid contributed to the costs; the girls first danced together, but men arrived later in the evening.

A special feast, the doctor's feast, was held for those who had helped transport the sick to hospital or to a doctor. In the early days, patients had to be carried to a boat and rowed to the doctors or, alternatively, the doctor had to be rowed to the patient.

Christmas

The most important feast was Christmas, which lasted from Christmas Eve for the whole twenty days of Yuletide until 13 January. At this time, people played cards or visited friends. No spinning-wheel rolled and no other textile implement was used. Folklore said that nothing should be knitted or woven for a sailor at this time because he might drown. Plenty of stories were told about what misfortune befell people who wore clothes made during Christmas. Clothes should have been made ready long before Christmas, because this was when one put on one's new clothes for the year ahead. Unready clothes could not then be finished because the trolls might steal them.

A few days before Christmas, all work tools were put away and the open smoky-room was cleaned from top to bottom. The roof-timbers were washed down by men since it was thought unbecoming for women to climb onto the rafters. The inner door was taken off its hinges and laid on the rafters so that the men could reach the soot-laden beams. Water and urine were used, together with sheep suet as a cleansing medium. The women washed down the walls and provided the farm boys with other cleaning materials. Then a meal of meat was cooked and everyone ate. In some cases a new earth floor was also laid, at this time of year, and people danced to stamp it solid.

There was no traditional way of celebrating Christmas but many people had taken to eating goose in the Danish fashion.

In the Northern Isles their speciality has been to have well-hung fish and a sheep's rectum filled with tallow or meat for Christmas Day – this revolting-sounding dish can be very tasty. Christmas presents were introduced only in 1925, while Christmas trees came into use only after the last war. Current traditions lean heavily on Danish customs, for few traditional observances exist.

On Christmas morning people got up early and greeted everyone they met outside. They sat down to a real breakfast, an uncommon event, consisting of a grand meal of bread and butter, dried lamb's meat, fresh mutton, sausages and Christmas cake. The church service began at noon and afterwards fresh or hung lamb was served with potatoes. Supper consisted of sweet soup made of angelica. The evening was spent quietly with the reading of religious books. Neither card-playing nor dancing were indulged in. Church was attended twice but the service at 4 p.m. was the most important: candles were burnt at the altar, in the candelabras and along the pews.

Boxing Day was more secular, yet there was either a proper church service at midday with the minister or a written sermon read by the deacon. The food was the same as the day before, but schnapps was served and a grand dance finished the evening.

One special feature of Christmas was the tradition of the Christmas horse, where someone dressed up with a horse's head and participated in the dances. His role was to tease the girls. Such traditions are also common in Celtic countries, such as Wales and Cornwall, where the hobby-horse also has fertility connections.

New Year

Nothing special was made of New Year until recently; the meal was well-hung fish and sheep's rectum stuffed with tallow. The only difference was that people also lit bonfires and fired off shotguns. Children were keen on bonfires and bursting sheep's bladders, like balloons, that were kept specially for this occasion. The association of fires and noise, at the time of the New Year, is a common way to mark the end of the year, and to drive away evil spirits.

Many modern innovations have been introduced since the

war, like going to church on New Year's Eve, firstly at 8 p.m.
but then at 11 p.m. so that the congregation was in church at
midnight, before the start of the new year. Many villages
nowadays light up their streets with oil-filled canisters when all
other lights are extinguished, just before midnight, so that the
place is lit only by flickering lamps. Other villages have
adopted the Scandinavian tradition of setting lighted candles
in their windows. Some villages have elaborate bonfires, complete with brass bands playing the New Year in, after which
people visit each other. In some places people even burn old
boats, as in Shetland, but these are very modern practices.

Tradition says that nobody should ever go to sleep before
the New Year is in, and so people kept awake, by whatever
means. It is related that, not so long ago, a man used to go out
with some pilot whale meat in both his hands while his sister
went out with a milk pail in her hand, to greet the New Year's
sun, in order to be lucky the whole year. New Year's Day was
an important dance day as well.

Winter dance days

Four other festivals were celebrated between Christmas and
Lent: Twelfth Night, Twentieth Night, Candlemas and
Shrove-tide. The important events were the dances, and different villages celebrated each of these four festivals in an
agreed way such that one village was responsible for Christmas, another for Twelfth Night, and so on. Most villages were
bound to each other in a network of feast relations, so that the
dances were alternately held in each other's village. It is said
that the Christmas and New Year celebrations were held only
in villages with churches. People from distant villages generally came the day before and stayed with their hosts, as they had
done for generations. Those from nearby villages just turned
up for the festivities in the evening.

These dance journeys were closely connected to the religious
life, for these feasts days were prominent occasions in the
Church calendar. It was the done thing to visit the church with
one's hosts and then eat dinner with them. In the evening the
dancing began and lasted until the small hours, but it was
always possible to take a break and call on friends, where the
men would be given a bit of bread and a nip – women were not

supposed to drink. The hosts would conduct their guests along their way home, and the day ended with a little ring-dance of farewell, out in the open.

These winter dances declined in popularity during this century, especially after the introduction of prohibition in 1907 that restricted the sale of alcohol. These dance journeys used to foster relationships between villages and often led to marriages that strengthened these ties. It should be remembered that these social activities occurred in a peasant economy and took place at a slack time of the agricultural year. Increasing wealth, due to fishing and, ironically, better communication, has seen the death of these traditional activities and so the dances are now only a leisure-time activity for a few interested groups.

Customs

It was a custom to have mummers at the beginning of Lent. Children and young people disguised themselves with masks, so as not to be recognized, and went from house to house. The hosts had to guess who they were, while the mummers did their best to distort their voices. At the end, the mummers received cakes, fruit and sweets. Today, only children dress up in this way.

In Miðvágur, there was a custom of a couple of young people dressing up as monsters and going round the houses. They blackened their faces and hung seaweed in their hair, as well as over the rags they wore. They would shriek and gesticulate wildly, so as to frighten the children. These mummers were often poor people, who had no other choice but to perform in this rather shameful way, as the purpose of these visits was to demand meat – at Lent!

At Midsummer, some young people used to go to the warm spring (*Varmakelda*), outside Fuglafjørður to dance. In other places, dancing also took place outside the village and away from the control of the parents.

Ólavsøka, on 29 July, was a time when the *ting* met in Tórshavn and people from all over the Faroes assembled here. The priesthood and MPs came together for worship in the town church. Crows' beaks, that all able-bodied men in the Faroes were compelled to bring, were burnt on Tinganes because this bird was considered a danger to the all-important sheep. During this century, Ólavsøka has expanded to include sporting activities like football, horse racing and boat racing.

Today, Ólavsøka attracts to Tórshavn thousands of visitors from other villages, who stay with friends and relatives. Public offices close down during this period. Parades in the flag-bedecked streets, and many sporting and cultural activities are the order of the day. This festival is not really for foreigners, as the whole purpose is to meet friends. Some people dress up in traditional costumes that are far too warm for their centrally-heated houses today, but are fine in the street when you are seeking out acquaintances. This is the time when you see a great amount of good-humoured public drunkenness. Sometimes, spontaneous Faroese dancing takes place in the streets but generally this is done in a private dance locale.

Special customs connected to birth, baptism, marriage and death were once observed but these are purely of historic interest nowadays. Most of the celebrations connected with these events can be thought of as winter festivities, despite the lapse of time between the event and its celebration. Birth and confirmation were not marked out in any particular way; marriages usually took place in the autumn, while the baptismal and funeral beers were often kept until the winter before they were consumed.

The Struggle for Independence

Romanticism

The disastrous war between Denmark and England (1807–14) led to the financial collapse of the Danish state and the imposition of the Treaty of Kiel, by which Denmark surrendered Norway to Sweden but still kept control of Iceland, Greenland and the Faroes. Only after the European revolutions of 1848 did the Danish king renounce his absolutism and allow the introduction of a new constitution in 1849, and of free trade in 1854.

What happened in the last quarter of the nineteenth century was a resurgence of national feelings in Iceland, the Faroes and Norway – the independent Viking spirit was aflame against their political masters. Ironically, these desires were fanned by students from these very three dependent countries meeting at the University of Copenhagen! The new spirit of the times was Romanticism, which was basically a literary movement in which the poet was to be a guide and prophet for the people. Not unnaturally, Romanticism had political overtones, but it was not exclusively liberal. If one thing characterized Romantic artists (poets, novelists and composers) it was *passion* – which could concern human love, nature or one's country. The Romantic poet's imagination was often stirred by the past as this allowed greater freedom to his art, in exploring a realm that was unconstrained by the present. In choosing his subject, it was only natural to find it among his own people and, in the spirit of nationalism of the times, it led to feelings of patriotism about a golden age – not simply one in the past, but one that was to come.

The position of Iceland and the Faroes, under the Danish Crown, was very similar politically and economically, and their languages were very similar, being basically Old Norse. However, they differed markedly in one chief respect – that Iceland developed a written language as early as the twelfth century whereas the Faroese script emerged only a mere century ago. Thus, Icelandic maintained its form of writing for almost nine centuries, largely uninfluenced by the changes undergone by the other Scandinavian countries.

The Faroese were quite unable to write down the verses of the ballads that they sang to the accompaniment of a ring-dance – both being derived from medieval French culture and probably brought to the Faroes by either Norwegian or Icelandic poets. These ballads concerned chivalric deeds like those of Charlemagne or heroic deeds of ancient Norsemen. This lack of writing may, paradoxically, have kept the memories of these ballads alive in the people's memories.

Antiquarianism

During the eighteenth-century Enlightenment, many learned societies flourished with the object of spreading knowledge to the populace at large, for practical and intellectual reasons. It was also an age of Antiquarianism where scholars delighted in looking at ancient things – old books and old objects.

It was a Danish scientist called H. C. Lyngbye who promoted the collection of more Faroese ballads. He came to the Faroes in 1817 to study coastal algae, but became interested in ballad dancing. In 1822 Lyngbye published a book – *Faroese ballads about Sigurd, the slayer of Fafnir, and his kin* – that was actually the first book to be published in Faroese. This event awoke the interest of other Scandinavian scholars in this ancient oral literature. Apart from the fact that these oral ballads were not widely seen in print, though known to the villagers, the basic problem still remained that nobody really knew how to spell this language properly.

Nationalism

This love of the past was increased by the Romantic movement, which praised the achievements of one's forebears.

Thus, the Enlightenment's desire for scientific knowledge fostered by the learned societies, combined with national pride, produced an explosion of scholarship and learning. The nineteenth century thus saw the emergence of nationalism, as peoples realized their different pasts and sought to emphasize their own, superior peculiarities.

Iceland had never accepted Denmark's rule willingly and continued to press for independence from the mid-eighteenth century onwards. This was not the case in the Faroes; the administration, the Church and eventually schooling had all been conducted in Danish since the Reformation and, indeed, continued thus until the Second World War. Only common speech and the ballads were conducted in Faroese, but these were considered to be simply corrupt dialects of Danish and Icelandic, according to the newly formed Roskilde Parliamentary Assembly of 1845 which decided that the proper language for school instruction in the Faroes should be Danish. Centuries of repression had left their mark on their self-esteem, and all that separated them, culturally, from their masters was their distinctive languages, oral and song traditions from the past, though these were generally despised as being backward and retrogressive. It was only the deep concern of Romantic antiquarians to 'save' these last remnants of culture from oblivion that changed matters.

The Faroese clergyman V. U. Hammershaimb (1819–1909), son of the former king's bailiff W. Hammershaimb, protested about the Roskilde Assembly's decision in 1845 about the compulsory use of Danish in Faroese schools, and he declared that Faroese was a language in its own right. However, to prove his point, he realized that he would have to devise an orthography, based on etymological principles, that was common to all Faroese dialects. To this end, he collaborated with an Icelandic scholar to devise a system that, essentially, is the one used to this day. He began publishing his findings on Faroese ballads, sayings and traditions from 1851 onwards. He later backed up his work with a systematic coverage of the language and literature of the Faroes, which he researched between 1886–91 with the help of his compatriot J. Jakobsen. These results were published as *Færøsk Anthologi* (Faroese Anthology) in 1891. Hammershaimb's early work had established Faroese as a language dealing with the literature of the old sagas, interesting from an antiquarian point of view, but not as a living language.

Nationalism in Denmark, Norway and Iceland came to fruition during an economic upswing, and so it was in the Faroes too. The abolition of the Royal Monopoly in 1856 allowed local merchants to indulge in free trade, but what had they to offer? Their goods were the same woollen goods as always, since the society was still agriculturally based. Iceland had always exploited fishing, and the expansion of her trade with the English (for whom the Icelanders fished and sold their catch) accounted for their recent economic boom; but this did not happen in the Faroes since the English already fished off the Faroes for themselves. Only after 1872 did the Faroese really learn to fish – using old English sloops! By the turn of the century, Faroese fishing off Iceland produced good returns in the spring and autumn fishing, and so the economy began to prosper – the old agricultural society gradually collapsed, and the fishing economy was the order of the day. The improved economic conditions produced a doubling of the population between 1800–80, and this increase also demanded the provision of more clergymen and trained persons; and so the numbers of students going to Copenhagen also increased, as the richer farmers and shopkeepers sent their sons south. Thus, by 1876, twelve Faroese students were in Copenhagen and they formed a student association, five years later, which they then celebrated by composing poems and patriotic songs in honour of their country. They published this collection as a songbook in 1892, but they did not use Hammershaimb's orthography but that of the young J. Jakobsen, Hammershaimb's collaborator, who used a more phonetically-based orthography.

The language issue

The Romantic ideals of these young Faroese students were brought back to the Faroes and given a political slant by a publicly-called folk meeting in 1888 that demanded the use of the Faroese language in religious matters, schooling and public affairs. The upshot of that meeting was the formation of the Faroese Union and the regular production of a newspaper called *Føringatiðindi* (The Faroese News) from 1890 to 1901, whose aim was to press for independence from Denmark. However, they could not agree on an acceptable orthography – the choice was between Hammershaimb's and Jakobsen's – and so the Union disintegrated, bitterly. Nevertheless, the wide readership of this newspaper was a key to the fact that the Faroese could begin to read and write in their own language, by the turn of the century.

The problems facing Faroese writers were threefold: which orthography to use, which words to employ and where to publish? After much debate it was agreed to use a modified version of Hammershaimb's orthography, despite (or because of) its similarity to written Icelandic. The question of vocabulary was a vexed one because the traditional words used in the ballads or in daily life were limited in number and tended to be concerned only with concrete and practical matters, rather than abstract ideas. Obviously, Danes had words for most ideas but to employ these was thought to be a betrayal of the mother tongue. Some writers opted out and wrote only in Danish while others strove to create new words by borrowing concepts from the well-established Icelandic vocabulary and also by ingenious combinations of old words. Gradually an accepted vocabulary was built up and a Faroese–Danish dictionary was compiled and published in 1928. With the rise of political parties at the turn of the century a need arose to form words expressing political ideals and practice.

Faroese literature

The first significant poet of any stature was J. H. O. Djurhuus (1881–1948), a Faroese lawyer who published his first poem in the Independence Party newspaper, *Tingakrossur* in 1901. His poems are drenched in Greek mythology, a thin disguise for his love of the Faroes. He actually translated the *Iliad* into Faroese, plus some of Plato's dialogues. Djurhuus was a lyric poet much concerned about his own soul and nature – seen through Faroese eyes.

J. H. O. Djurhuus' younger brother, H. A. Djurhuus (1883 –1951), was a teacher and tried his hand at many forms of writing: poems, psalms, nursery rhymes, stories and plays. All these proved to be very popular, as they were romantically conceived and solely concerned with the Faroes.

While also writing poems, J. Dahl trained to be a teacher but became a minister and eventually Dean of the Faroes. Amongst his many accomplishments was the translation of the *New Testament* (1937) into Faroese, besides many psalms (1921), a service book (1930), a general prayer book (1939) and many other religious works. Not surprisingly, Dahl, with his love of the Faroese language, won great support from those who wished for independence from Danish rule, and this was, in a sense, also a political victory.

The key figure in this whole saga of Faroese political independence and the triumph of the Faroese language was Jóannes Patursson (1866–1946). He was the largest Crown-farmer in the Faroes, at the ancient religious centre of Kirkjubøur, south of Tórshavn. He trained at a Norwegian College of Agriculture and imbibed some of their political and linguistic ideals. He was a poet in the traditional ballad idiom as well as the new lyric style. He edited *Føringatíðindi* but quarrelled over the orthography. He singlehandedly set up the Independence party and went on to be a member of the Danish parliament and the Faroese *Løgting*. He contributed widely to local newspapers in his endeavour to win complete independence for the Faroes in all matters.

It can be seen from this short account that Faroese literature was launched by just a dozen or so prominent men between 1890 and 1915. Another dozen writers also contributed, but the point is that their numbers were extremely small in relation to the total population of 12,000.

The period 1915–45 saw the continuation of the old guard of writers, but a gradual diminution of lyric poetry occurred with a rise in prose works. The most important figures of this period were Heðin Brú (1901–87) and William Heinesen (1900–) who were both novelists; Brú wrote in Faroese but Heinesen wrote in Danish. They both wrote about the past conditions in the Faroes and each has written a dozen first-class novels.

Since the war many earlier writings have been published for the first time. Poetry continues but it is not so lyrical and is more modernistic. Novels and village histories are still produced by the score.

The rise of political parties

The fateful combination of young intellectuals and impover-
ished landless farm-workers at the close of the nineteenth
century produced a strong desire for a new order based on
universal equal rights. Although their aims were not quite the
same, they both detested the current order. The students
wished to be equal to the Danish officials who had lorded it
over them, and the workers wanted to be as good as their
masters. The political party that most nearly met both these
ideals was the Danish Left party – a Liberal party. In the 1901
Danish elections, a landslide Liberal victory returned the
Faroese candidate – Jóannes Patursson, son of a Faroese
Crown-farmer, Norwegian-trained, and married to an Ice-
lander. Not surprisingly, as a nationalist, he wanted Home
Rule for the Faroes! He continued with this cause in the next
election too, but then overplayed his hand by demanding that
the Faroese *Løgting* should have complete control over all the
revenue raised and spent in the Faroes! The merchants and
officials panicked at this thought because, at that time, it cost
the Danish Exchequer far more to service the Faroes than they
ever got back in revenue.

Patursson lost the next election. His victorious opponents
then formed themselves into the *Samband* (Unionist) party,
devoted to retaining ties with Denmark, but also to keeping
internal finances under control. Patursson's minority sup-
porters in the *Løgting* then banded themselves together as the
Sjálvstýri (Home Rule) party. It was from such personal
animosities that Faroese politics began to develop in the early
twentieth century. Despite the emotional appeal of Faroese
independence, the Unionist party retained their overall majority up to the end of the First World War. The population had
by then reached 20,000, while exports of fish had reached
record proportions; but the distribution of wealth was still
grossly unequal. This situation led to inescapable confronta-
tions between the shipowners and the fishermen. It is, therefore, not surprising that during the inter-war period, when
fishing became the most important factor and with the industry suffering a recession, that attention was concentrated more
on economic matters than political matters. Considerations of

complete Home Rule had to wait until there was a sufficient economic base.

A mutual insurance scheme, a trading bank and government assistance towards the purchase of boats proved highly successful and the fishing fleet grew from strength to strength. One consequence of this increased activity was an increasing polarization between shipowners and fishermen, in the early decades of this century, over terms of employment which led to the formation of an association of employers and a trade union.

This rise of an industrial sector in the economy paved the way for the setting up of the Faroese Social Democratic party (*Javnaðarflokkurin*) in 1925 which was eventually to clip the wings of the Unionist and Independence parties. However, another new party was formed in 1936 – the Economic party (*Vinnuflokkurin*) – which opposed the policies of the Social Democrats. The Economic party was founded by businessmen who had recently set up the private bank – *Sjóvinnubankin* (The Fishery Industry Bank) – which aimed to promote native resources and initiatives. In 1939 a new development happened – the formation of another new party: The People's party (*Folkaflokkurin*). This arose from a move to allow poor fishermen to have allotments in the outfield of Crown-farms to grow food, since the fishing was in recession. But J. Patursson, the leader of the Independence party, objected as he happened, ironically, to be the largest Crown-farmer! So, Patursson joined forces with the Economic party and they founded the People's party which was to have great popular support during the Second World War.

Just before the outbreak of war, Denmark was persuaded to allow the use of Faroese in the schools and churches. This new equality of Faroese and Danish was probably due less to political pressure than to the obvious fact that a respectable body of Faroese literature was there to prove that it was a viable language.

Denmark capitulated to Germany on 9 April 1940. Three days later the British occupied the Faroes and, a month later, Iceland as well. The outcome of this severance from Denmark led to a declaration of independence on the part of Iceland in June 1944. In the Faroes, a referendum was held in September 1946 to decide whether or not to secede from Denmark; the result was inconclusive even though a slight majority was in favour of secession. After much discussion, an Act of Parliament was promulgated to take effect on 1 April 1948 that defined the Faroes as a self-governing community within the Danish kingdom.

The Faroes left the war with a handsome balance of payments surplus for running fish to Britain and with the feeling that they could run their own affairs quite well by themselves. An additional boost to national pride was the British ordinance that Faroese ships must fly not the Danish flag but the Faroese flag – invented by a group of Faroese students way back in 1919 but never officially allowed before. With their language officially acknowledged, with money and a national flag, the time seemed ripe for complete independence from Denmark. However, the various political parties could not agree. Matters were made more complicated by the emergence of yet another party in 1948 the Republican party (*Tjóðveldisflokkurin*) – led by the son of J. Patursson who objected to the Home Rule Act being imposed on the Faroes.

III THE CURRENT POLITICAL AND SOCIAL SETTING

12 Present-day Life (1949–89)

The Home Rule Act

In the last chapter we traced how the movement for independence culminated in granting the Faroes a limited degree of self-determination with the Home Rule Act of 1948. This Act set the guidelines for the future development of the islands which defined the Faroes as a self-governing community within the Danish kingdom according to the law. The post of *Amtmand*, or Governor, was abolished and replaced by a *Rigsombudsmand*, or High Commissioner. The new local authorities were to be the *Løgting*, or legislative assembly, and the *Landstýri*, or government. The Faroese language and flag were officially recognized but Danish could also be used in official communications and should be taught in schools. The islands were to be part of the Danish currency area and the Faroese currency was to be kept on par with the Danish kroner.

The Act also set out the various areas of responsibility, under two headings: *A)* those that might be taken over by the Faroese administration at any time, on request; *B)* those items of joint responsibility that might be taken over from Denmark, after negotiations. As can be imagined many areas have been gradually taken over in the last forty years. So far, the Faroese government has taken over most of the administrative responsibilities from List A except for social insurance, the health service and education. From List B, the Faroese government has taken over the radio and television, the agricultural fund, import- and export-control. Other items remaining are the

Church, police, sub-surface resources (now under discussion) and air traffic. However, the areas of justice, finance, defence and foreign affairs may *not* be taken over. The penal code, civil law, company law and insurance are covered by Danish legislation, but these laws do not automatically come into effect in the Faroes, since the *Løgting* must first give its consent; hence most Acts introduced into the Danish Parliament often have the rider 'except in the Faroes'. Thus the Faroes have gained a great degree of freedom, but all these areas of responsibility that have been taken over have to be paid for out of taxes and duties.

The public authorities are, then, the Home Government (*Landstýri*), comprising 3 to 6 members headed by the Prime Minister (*Løgmaður*) who are chosen by the Parliament (*Løgting*), as well as including the *kommuner* and the State. The *Løgting* has 27 members, chosen from 7 constituencies, plus 5 extra seats that are used to ensure proportional representation, and hence its numbers can vary between 27 and 32. The 50 local authorities have a large amount of autonomy but they do cooperate with regard to health and education provision, as well as for local roads and harbours. The State is represented by the High Commissioner (*Rigsombudsmand*) who has the right to speak in the Parliament, besides a local judge and a chief constable.

Political parties

The political parties represented in the *Løgting* fall into five separate groupings that reflect their different attitudes on two major issues: 1) the usual Right/Left division on social and economic matters; 2) the relationship to Denmark – Union/ Independence. This may be shown thus:

INDEPENDENCE

Republicans   People's party

LEFT   Home Rule party/   RIGHT
Christian People's party

Social Democrats   Unionist party

UNION

Roykstova: These 'smoky-rooms' were the central work-place in a house since this was where the fire was. As there was no chimney but only a lum, these rooms became filled with peat smoke. This example comes from the crown-farm in Kirkjubøur. The objects on the stove are obvious except for the wool-carders on the right. To the left, against the wall are various agricultural implements. These things would not have been found here in this position in the olden days. See Chapter 14.

Island Life

Blásastova Museum: This 'glass-room' is at Norðragøta: it was the fine room where the minister might stay. See Chapter 15.

Kalvalið: This famous dwelling was characteristic of the period, fitting snuggly into the hillside. Note the single window of the '*glas-stova*'. See Chapter 17, Miðvágur.

Women's national costume: Traditional female dress is strikingly colourful. A black cape, lined in crimson, is the outer garment. The bodice is red with silver ornaments. The skirt is red with black stripes. Sometimes, an embroidered or plain woollen shawl is thrown across the shoulders. Everyone has an embroidered apron whose design varies with the village of origin. These costumes are extremely warm and were perfectly adapted to the old society but are far too warm to wear inside today with central heating: they are only worn for outside use, nowadays.

National costumes: Male costume consists of knickerbockers with silver buttons, a knitted sweater with silver buttons, a red waistcoat with silver buttons and a woven red forage-cap [if young] but a blue hat [if old]. Both men and women wear black shoes with silver buckles, if traditionally dressed.

The Magnus Cathedral: This photo shows the black crown-farm building at Kirkjubøur to the left and the grey walls of the cathedral to the right. See Chapter 14.

Funningur church: This elaborate rood-screen
is typical of many of the old-fashioned churches
– plain, carved wood in traditional patterns.
See Chapter 15.

Haldarsvík church: Despite its modern
appearance this church is over 130 years old.
See Chapter 15.

Tórshavn, old church: Incidentally, this snow
fell in June! To the left you can see the copper,
pyramidical top of Vesturkirkjan.

Elections to the *Løgting* are normally every four years. The Home Government is, as usual, made up of a coalition and is currently (1990) represented by members from the People's party, the Home Rule party, the Republicans and the Progress party, but headed by the People's party. The Faroese also send two representatives to the Danish Parliament, the *Folketing*. These two MPs, ironically, often play a critical role in deciding the fate of the Danish Government, which is often in a perilous coalition itself.

All post-war Faroese governments have been coalitions between three of the five main political parties. The Unionist and Social Democrats have taken turns to provide the leadership, and while they are at different ends of the political spectrum they were united in wishing to retain ties with Denmark. The equally diverse independent parties: People's, Independence and Republican parties have had only a brief period of office between 1963–7 when they disappointed both the radical and conservative voters and were not to form a subsequent government until 1989. The chief concern of all governments has been the fishing industry since this is their only lifeline. This concern led to the gradual extension of the fishing limits from 3 to 200 miles, following Icelandic precedents. A consequence of other nations taking the same action meant that the Faroese had to negotiate agreements about where to fish and also how much they could catch.

Trading and the infrastructure

At the end of the war, with a sizeable sterling balance, the Faroese were determined to use this capital to further their prosperity by investing in trawlers, instead of using their old wooden sloops. Again, Britain was willing to sell them old steam trawlers at a cheap price, since they were now turning to diesel trawlers! Villages vied with each other to get a steam trawler of their own. Initially, things went well but then things began to fall apart – like the obsolete trawlers themselves. Rising coal prices, devaluation of the pound, the Korean war and increasing competition sent many businesses into bankruptcy. The Fishery Industry Bank (*Sjóvinnubankin*), that had invested heavily in the trawler fleet, suddenly collapsed in 1951. The *Løgting* immediately set up a committee to examine

which were the most profitable boats with which to recon-
struct the Faroese fishing fleet. The answer was long-line boats,
but the problem was the expense.

Rescue eventually came with the setting up of the Faroe
Islands Mortgage Finance Corporation in 1955, which orig-
inated from Marshall Aid. This corporation enabled owners to
finance the building of boats, with a small deposit of just 10 per
cent of their own money, plus government loans. The effect
was dramatic as the whole fleet was completely reconstructed
within ten years. Fish catches almost doubled during this
period.

An important infrastructural change was the introduction in
1953 of a public electricity supply to the main islands. This
was designed to stimulate the various demands of the fishing
industry, from shipbuilding and repair to fish processing. At
the same time, the Faroese government pressed ahead with the
building of roads and harbours. This activity received a massive boost in 1964 with the setting up of the Danish Investment
Fund for the Faroe Islands, which coordinated public investment in large-scale infrastructural improvements. This was a
yearly rolling fund of some 10 million kr. that, over the years,
has radically modernized the whole transport system from
roads to harbour facilities.

The Faroese balance of trade has rarely been positive but it
was not very serious until 1973 when the combination of
inflation, large imports and loans set the country on the path of
ever-increasing debt. The responsibility for this lay with the
government of the day, the Social Democrats, who believed
that they could spend their way out of the recession. Big loans
were taken to invest in modernizing the telephone system
and improving roads and harbours. The *kommuner* (local
councils) were swept along by these schemes and also started
borrowing money to create local work by extending their
harbours and setting up fish factories. While some of this
financial credit was obtained from Danish banks and institutions, both the government and the *kommuner* also went to
foreign countries to get loans. The debts spiralled, causing a
crisis in the early 80s, and a Conservative government was
returned after a surprise election in mid-term. The grave
financial situation, unsurprisingly, did not improve during
these four years of Right-wing rule and so a Left-wing

government was returned in 1985 to cope with the biggest trade deficit ever: 1 million kr. – as large as the total exports from the Faroes in 1980! It failed, and a Right wing government was returned in 1988 with a policy of fierce retrenchment. Meanwhile the net foreign debt had soared from 1,500 million in 1982 to over 8,000 million kr. in 1989.

These figures are mentioned to stress the point that the Faroes are becoming more and more dependent on outside finance to keep their economy rolling. As they take on more and more responsibilities from Denmark, they equally have to pay for them, and this effectively ties them even closer to Denmark financially.

International relations and the local economy

Foreign relations are the responsibility of the Danish Government but the Home Government can negotiate on matters of interest to the Faroes, with the assistance of the Foreign Ministry. While the Faroes are included in Denmark's membership of the UN and NATO, this does not automatically include economic matters. The other Nordic countries retained their EFTA exemptions on Faroese goods. These agreements were critically vital if the Faroes were ever going to compete on the European market against the other fishing nations.

International organizations set the quotas of fish that may be caught in the Atlantic and the North Sea areas. The Faroes have also entered into bilateral agreements for reciprocal fishing rights with other nations, such as the USSR, Norway, Iceland and those in the EEC.

Despite the increasing negative balance of trade over the years there has been little unemployment so far and, indeed, people from other countries have been coming in to do temporary work in the fishing industry and construction work. The large external debts still have to be paid for, and, in recent years, a tendency has been to seek more overseas loans to pay these off. The Faroese have been very prosperous on this borrowed money up to now, but times of change are at hand. The 1989 fishing season was disastrous, as the fleet failed to catch sufficient fish to make it economical to attempt to go out. The combined effect of international quotas and over-fishing the trash fish, that are the real basis of the food chain for commercial fishing, has spelled ruin and unemployment. So the Faroese are in a dilemma today: they have to service their debts yet the very foundation of their economy – fishing – is proving unreliable. The Faroese are a resourceful nation but they are facing one of their most serious challenges so far. One solution may be to invest in tourism since they have some of the most attractive scenery in the North Atlantic.

Attitudes towards religion

Perhaps the biggest cultural change in the Faroes during this last century has been people's attitude towards religion. As in many peasant societies, the Church once played a major role in inculcating values and explaining the vicissitudes of life, but as agriculture gave way to fishing, the traditional association of the Church and farming weakened and both lost status.

Although the Faroese were devout Lutherans and even sang hymns as they used to row out to fish, or went to gather birds' eggs on the cliffs – both risky undertakings – these practices died out earlier this century. A more dynamic religion was introduced 100 years ago from Scotland that had a special appeal to poor fishermen: this was the Plymouth Brethren sect. The Brethren are fundamentalist and hold to adult baptism, which means that one is not born into the sect but becomes a member, voluntarily, and this enabled the sect to recruit from the lackadaisical Lutherans. They had great success in the Northern Isles, where fishing activity was at its greatest in the Faroes, earlier this century. The Brethren had appeal because it gave these poor fishermen the status denied them by the farming communities. They kept to themselves and only had dealings with each other – Brethren would fish and trade only with each other. So successful were the Brethren in their economic activities that they now constitute 10 per cent of the population and are among the richest people in the Faroes today. This makes them the natural allies of the People's party. The traditional Unionist party can appeal only to farmers and Lutherans, while the other parties tend to be agnostic.

The Faroes are not as completely secularized as the rest of Scandinavia, but religious faith is waning as the standard of living rises. The attitude towards the past and one's ethnic roots is also ambivalent. The old farming community centred on the Church and its rituals, when people dressed up in their peasant costumes, is a thing of the past – just as the ballads and ring-dances are on festival occasions. Today, a revival of peasant costume for national events has emerged while amateur societies painfully commit to memory the old dances and ballads, but this is more for entertainment than an expression of any deeply-felt ethnic identity.

Social change: a personal digression

Social change has happened so quickly that there is a double generation gap in the Faroes between those people who still remember the earlier days of this century and their children who lived in the war period, and between these children and their adult grandchildren, to whom the present world has always been like it is now. In other words, three different and incompatible sets of impressions of Faroese social life are held by different generations.

I have a theory that people always interpret their current world in terms of the way in which they came to understand things when they reached intellectual maturity at twenty-six years of age, and so their insights, then, determine the way in which they will interpret the present, as well as all past events and future affairs. From close observation of Faroese of all ages, I have been constantly struck at how well my hypothesis seems to stand up when questioning people about their views about the dramatic social changes that have occurred this century. A favourable plausibility about this idea struck me, when trying to understand the varying accounts given of the same events in the past and the present, by considering them in terms of an individual's own biography. Here, the family background, religion, politics, present occupation and their ambitions present a profile that can be checked against age. This aside, it suggests that accounts of the past, given by different informants, should always be compared, with regard to their 'fixated' age, and in terms of the social conditions at that particular time.

It is worth recalling that during the Second World War, many people were still living in small turf-roofed houses, heated by peat, lit by oil lamps, and wholly fed from their potato patch, the family cow, the outfield sheep, the fish from the spring and autumn catches, as well as their share of the occasional pilot whale catch. Such conditions had existed before the 1880s and also well within the active memory of most inhabitants. Basically, very little change in living conditions had occurred since the first settlement of the Faroes, apart from the relatively recent introduction of the potato and the regular off-shore fishing trips. The actual pattern of life had not really altered significantly for more than a millennium!

Compare that picture, 40 years ago, with today's homes: spacious, timber-built Scandinavian-imported, roof-tiled houses, centrally-heated, lit electrically, and fed from the freezer, complete with hi-fi, television and video. This is an obvious exaggeration, of course, since only the young professionals can afford all these luxuries, but the future pattern is there! Although most Faroese own their own homes, there is a paradox here, because whilst the older generation simply inherited their parents' homes and gradually modernized them, the young 30-year-olds build expensive new homes and offset their mortgages against their taxes. The general feeling is that 'Denmark will pay!' – to parody the war-time feeling that 'Britain would pay'. Such cynical thoughts, in truth, underlie much of the Faroese attitude towards money matters in the long run.

The picture I wish to conjure up is a basic disjunction between the older generation's attitude of pay-as-you-go and today's younger generation's attitude that the future will take care of itself – with Denmark's help.

So my hypothesis is that those who came to 'enlightenment' during good economic times such as the 60s onwards – i.e. those who were born between 1934 and 1960 – are likely to be optimistic about the future. This is a third of the total population, but all those born since 1934 also account for *half* the present voting population. This speculation of mine might account for the fairly even split between the 'progressivists' and the 'traditionalists' in recent years, since the older generation of voters were also equally split depending on whether they had experienced good or bad times. In this division of opinion we also see the political aspirations of the independents and unionists.

This explanation of attitudes might suggest why an ambivalence is present in the Faroese views about independence and dependence, the old customs and the new. The older generation knew they could not be politically independent despite their cultural differences from Denmark since their recently invented culture was an insufficient base from which to declare unilateral and complete independence. Some of the younger and more confident generation believed that cultural differences and possible financial self-sufficiency are sufficient grounds for separation. The lines of action are equally divided between going-it-alone and relying on more powerful friends. This stalemate in attitudes led inexorably towards improving the status quo that, inevitably, meant borrowing capital from outside to make good their dreams.

The power of the media

An important determinant of people's attitudes nowadays is the media. Newspapers foster an inward-looking attitude that focuses almost exclusively on things Faroese. The two other important media are radio (started in 1957) and television (begun in 1984) that send out very contradictory messages to the Faroese people.

Local radio (*Utvarp Føroya*) is entirely in Faroese and it broadcasts news and current affairs programmes, though for most of the day it just sends out popular music. News programmes take up a fifth of the transmission time. The main evening news is at 6.30 p.m. and consists of the weather, local news, besides announcements of birthdays, funerals, concerts, talks and other events. Everyone listens to this programme because there are no regular daily newspapers. At this, and at other news spots, the most important item of news is the daily fishing catch. Villages vie with each other for the best results and the competition is followed more eagerly than the successes of their respective football teams. Thus the evening news is a national event that keeps everyone *au fait* with what is happening in the various villages. Radio, then, can be said to have a centripetal effect of uniting the people together into one big community.

Television (*Sjónvarp Føroya*) has completely the opposite effect to radio – it disrupts the sense of community. In 1989 broadcasts were on Tuesdays, Thursdays and Fridays between

7.30 and 11.30 p.m. as well as afternoon and evening trans-
missions at the weekend. Just three news programmes are
shown each week, compiled mainly from tapes flown in from
Danish Radio, but BBC news items may also be included. In
addition, satellite television is now available and receiving
dishes are found almost everywhere.

The effect of television on leisure time is well known: it
isolates. More significantly, it opens up the whole world to
your gaze and diminishes feelings towards the local environ-
ment. The Faroese are now exposed to political reporting, but
it is about the doings of unknown MPs in the Danish Parliament. Thus, television trivializes what is going on at home,
reduces local loyalties, boosts the importance of Denmark
and, naturally, the Unionist parties.

A sense of identity

It can be seen that the Faroese case of cultural ethnicity and
social identity is a complex one. There is little doubt that today
the Faroese are proud of the unique identity that they have
created. Internally, in the islands their common identity is
redundant except to distinguish themselves from the Danes,
but it is with the increasing contact with other nationals due to
bilateral fishing agreements, etc. that the Faroese identity
becomes important. It is both the richness of the Faroese
waters and the sheer efficiency of the Faroese fishing industry
that has thrust the Faroes into prominence in these economic
negotiations and strengthened their national image and pride.
Their heightened profile, in this sphere, may have also encouraged them to believe that they were quite capable of determin-
ing their own political fate: a Cinderella complex?

This wide-ranging survey of the multiple strands that came
together to form Faroese ethnicity has parallels with other
Scandinavian countries where certain groups have also thrown
off the cultural dominance of their more powerful neighbours.
Actual political independence is more generally the outcome of
wars, rather than revolutions, but it still needs to be coupled
with a strong, separate economic base for it to succeed. This is
the chief problem facing Eastern Europe today.

Conclusion

The Faroese have made significant gains this century in estab-
lishing their own ethnic identity, which is now unchallenge-
able. At the same time, a total change in the social ranking has
taken place: the once superior Crown-farmers and Danish
officials of the 1880s are now near the bottom of the heap,
while the formerly despised fishermen are towards the top of
the hierarchy today! As in Europe, generally, the new middle
classes of professionals have gained control. The cumulative
consequence of the mortgaging of the future has not yet been
fully realized since, politically, it thrusts the Faroese into ever-
increasing dependence on their backers – Denmark! Meanwhile, independence recedes further into the dark indefinite
future.

This assessment of the Faroes shows some of the limitations
that hedge in ethnic aspirations for complete political independence when the future economy is uncertain and unreliable. Perhaps the Faroese have now reached the acme of
their self-determination in the 1990s after this century of
struggle.

It is appropriate to conclude this historical and current
account of the Faroes by returning to the first chapter on the
land and sea because these two opposing factors played a
decisive role in the development of their society. In the first
millennium of occupation, it was the possession of land by
chiefs, the Church and Crown-farmers that determined everything. Land, however, was limited and this also limited
population and economic growth. The introduction of free
trade in the mid-nineteenth century opened up the possibility
of exploiting a new, free resource in the sea, that was apparently unlimited. This century-old period saw the rise to power
of merchants and fishermen, with a corresponding rise in
population and economic growth. The gradual realization that
limits to such growth were being forced on the Faroese, with
the introduction of international fishing-limits and quotas, has
led to a rude awakening and the present economic crisis. No
easy solution exists because the current possession of the sea is
no guarantee that the fish will always be there. The only
temporary avenue of escape is to claim the sub-surface rights in
both land and sea, where there might be exploitable mineral

wealth in the form of gas, oil and metals. So we have reached the final frontier – downwards!

As the Danes are unlikely to concede these sub-surface rights to the Faroese, as a matter of course, it seems possible that the Faroes will be drawn into even greater dependency on Denmark, economically and financially, while their cultural life (via television) will inevitably become more Danicized and cosmopolitan. Nevertheless, the Faroese have established a distinctive identity for themselves this century and can look back in pride on their achievements in making their small country into a worthy nation in the world community.

IV A TOUR THROUGH THE ISLANDS

This section contains twenty-six tourist trails that take you to all the villages in the islands. The capital, Tórshavn, has a chapter to itself. The trails radiate from just six centres on six different islands; they are Tórshavn (Streymoy), Sundalags-brúgvin (Eysturoy), Klaksvík (Borðoy), Oyrargjógv (Vágar), Skopun (Sandoy) and Vágur (Suðuroy).

For the sake of convenience, the trails are labelled alphabetically from A to Z. At the beginning of each chapter there is a list of the trails and accompanying maps which give the names of the villages to be visited, the distances between them in km (10 km = 6 English miles), the road numbers as well as page references to the text. It is not necessary to begin your excursions from these fixed points, of course, for they are merely convenient reference points in planning your trips.

Distances are not very great and so you can travel at leisure, but remember that ferries are prompt. If you are using public transport, be careful to check arrival and departure times because there are no guaranteed connections between buses and ferries.

A road sign marks the beginning of the village, like all other villages, announcing its name and that it is a built-up area demanding speed restrictions. The latter is shown by a silhouette of houses and everyone then knows that the speed limit is down to 50 km/hr (30 mph).

13   Tórshavn: the Capital

Tórshavn is the political, economic and cultural centre of the Faroes as well as being the hub of the transport system. This predominance is due to its central geographical location at the southern end of Streymoy. It is also dominant in the sense that a third of the population, i.e. 16,000, live in the broad sloping valley between Húsareyn (347 m) in the west and Kirkjubøreyn (350 m) to the south.

The origins of Tórshavn are traced to the rocky promontory (Tinganes) that divides the eastern from the western bay in the harbour, for it was determined early on in Viking times (c. AD 900) that the main *ting*, *Alting* (Parliament), should be held just here because of its central position in the Faroes. The oldest surviving medieval building (fourteenth-century) is *Munkastovan* (the Monk's Dwelling) which was used as a tithe barn. Next door is the sixteenth-century *Leigubúðin* (the Royal Rent-collection Store). Most of the other early buildings were destroyed in a fire in 1673, but it is ironic that the two tax-offices still survive to this day!

In 1580 the freebooter Magnus Heinason built a fort (*Skansin*) opposite Tinganes to protect the warehouses against pirates. A series of forts were built over the centuries but none of them proved very effective. However, the necessity to have permanent soldiers and workers would have led to a settlement, presumably near the east bay where the river flows out. At the beginning of the seventeenth century about 100 people lived there, but that total had tripled by the end of the century. Meanwhile the number of buildings on Tinganes also multiplied until some twenty were found there before the fire of 1673.

TÓRSHAVN

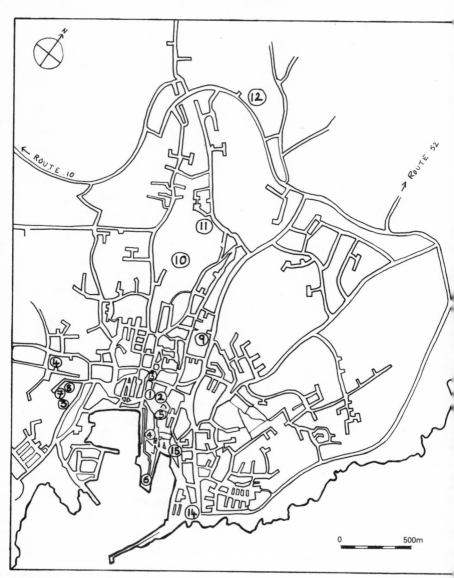

MAP INDEX

1. TOWN HALL
2. HOUSE OF PARLIAMENT
3. LIBRARIES

4. CHURCHES
5. HIGH COMMISSIONERS OFFICE

6. GOVERNMENT OFFICES
7. MUSEUMS
8. UNIVERSITY

9. SMS SHOPPING CENTRE
10. VIÐALUNDIN PARK

11. LISTASKÁLINN ART GALLERY
12. NORDIC HOUSE
13. HELIPAD

14. SKANSIN FORTIFICATION
15. FAROESE TOURIST BOARD

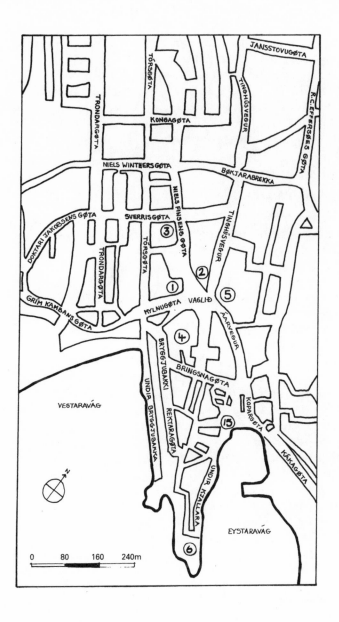

JANSSTOVUGØTA

TÓRSGØTA

TINGHÚSVEGUR

R.C.EFFERSØES GØTA

TRONDARGØTA

KONGAGØTA

NIELS WINTHERSGØTA

BØKJARABREKKA

DOKTARI JAKOBSENS GØTA

SVERRISGØTA

NIELS FINSENS GØTA

③

TINGHÚSVEGUR

TRONDARGØTA

TÓRSGØTA

②

GRÍM KAMBANS GØTA

①

MYLNUGØTA VAGLIÐ

⑤

AARVEGUR

④

BRYGGJUBAKKI

BRINGSNAGØTA

VESTARAVÁG

UNDIR ØRYGGJUBANKA

REKTARAGØTA

KOPARGØTA

⑮

KÁKAGØTA

N

UNDIR KJALLARA

EYSTARAVÁG

0   80   160   240m

⑥

By the time of the 1801 census the population of Tórshavn had grown to 554, from a total Faroese population of 5,265. The explosion in Tórshavn's population really began in 1945 when it had reached 4,400 people, doubled this in the twenty years to 1965 and doubled it yet again in the next twenty years. These increases were often to the detriment of smaller villages who lost their young people to Tórshavn, in search of better jobs.

The harbour area

For a sea-going people, the obvious focus of any village is the harbour. The harbour of the capital of the Faroes is the very nexus of the communication system. However, photographs from a century ago show only some old buildings tightly packed on the peninsula of Tinganes with boat-houses around the rocky shore of the eastern bay (*Eysteravág*), for there was no protective mole then, nor quays. The small rowing boats of the period were simply drawn up on the shore.

Today the harbour is a hive of activity, day and night. A half-km long mole protects the inner harbour while, outside it, is the container terminal. The larger car ferries coming from home and abroad, like *Norröna*, *Smyril* and *Teistin*, dock alongside the mole, while smaller car ferries such as *Tróndur* squeeze into the corner of the quaysides to unload. Cargo boats like *Blikur* and *Lómur* off-load their goods at the north-western quay where the small ferry boat *Ritan*, plying between Tórshavn and Nólsoy, docks. A small, neat marina jam-packed with colourful little boats is at the end of the eastern bay, but a much larger one lies in the western bay (*Vestaravág*) where there is also a shipbuilding and repair yard plus a large fish processing factory, *Bacalao*.

On a high grassy promontory overlooking the harbour is the fortress (*Skansin*) built to defend Tinganes and its warehouses. It has been rebuilt many times but has rarely fulfilled its promise since it was generally surrendered. The present shape dates from 1790 and was used as the headquarters of the British occupation forces in the last war. Its high position well serves the lighthouse that acts as a beacon to the many incoming vessels.

Tinganes is just a rocky split of land dividing the harbour

into two bays and is well worth a protracted visit since the buildings there represent the real heart of the old Tórshavn. Tinganes conveys a feeling of what things were like at the turn of the century better than any other place in the Faroes since it has been so well preserved.

At the neck of the promontory, a maze of little lanes run up between small, black dwelling-houses, interspersed with a few modern buildings and also some renovated old ones. Unfortunately for the visitor, these historic buildings have no signs on them to tell you which is which but you will find a good guide in the small booklet on Tinganes by A. Thorsteinsson.

At the end of the spit, is a three-storey, brown-timbered building called the Fort Warehouse (*Skansapakkhúsið*) which was erected in 1749 on the site of an earlier fort. Today it functions as the seat of the Home Government. Next door is The Great Hall (*Salurin*) which dates from 1781 and is on the site of The Old Store that was destroyed in the fire of 1673. This brown-timbered building is also a government office today. Adjoining them were two Monopoly warehouses that were burned down in an arson attack in 1950 but have been partially rebuilt. Further along on the west side are three more old buildings. The first is the Store Warehouse (*Bakkapakkhúsið*) built of timber in 1776 as an extension of the Royal Rent-collection Store (*Leigubúðin*) which was erected in 1619 for the collection of the king's rent, which was paid in kind. Next door is the Monk's Dwelling (*Munkastovan*), dating back to the Middle Ages and built with heavy stone walls, like those at Kirkjubøur; this construction enabled it to survive the devastating fire of 1673 that destroyed much of Tinganes.

On the eastern side of Tinganes is another row of buildings. Opposite the Great Hall is the Log Building (*Stokkastovan*), built after the 1673 fire, and its huge black timbers are joined in dovetail fashion which was most unusual for the Faroes. Next is the Dwelling House (*Sethúsini*), also erected after 1673, which was the trading-post manager's residence. A little further up is the Brewery (*Bryggihúsið*) which was timber-built in 1776. Beyond that is the Guard House (*Portugálið* – a linguistic distortion of *Corps de Garde*), a brick-built jail-house put up in 1693, as the crowned monogram of Christian V and the name of his feudal representative, F. v. Gabel, indicate. In 1762 this building was rebuilt as a two-storied, stone-walled building, to which an additional wooden storey was later added. Finally, at the head of this row of old buildings is the old vicarage of Reynagarður which was built as a four-winged farmhouse round an open paved courtyard in 1630. This building seems to have been Danish-inspired to judge from the construction, seen in the recently restored west wing. The east wing was demolished in 1820 and rebuilt in the Danish style, as was the north wing, with dovetail joints. The south wing was made with the standard Faroese stave technique of the 1600s. Not surprisingly, this vicarage stood next to the church in those days, but the latter was demolished in 1788 after a new church had been erected on its present site, to the north of Tinganes.

Havnar kirkja was built in 1788 in the traditional church style that we still find in Kaldbak, Hvalvík and Gøta, with black-timbered walls, a turf roof and a white spire. It was radically rebuilt in 1865, taking on its present shape: white on the outside but multicoloured within, a slate roof and an impressive clock tower. Over 600 worshippers may be accommodated in the nave and on the balconies. The church is rich with votive gifts: paintings, silver objects, bells and model boats – all given in thanksgiving from the seventeenth century onwards. At Ólavsøka (29 July) the Parliament is opened with a service and all the MPs, clergy and the High Commissioner process from the Løgtingshús to the church on that day.

The central area

Beginning at the harbour, near the modernistic façade of the Fishery Bank (*Sjóvinnubankin*) and past the little old houses in Gongin, is a road, Áarvegur, that leads to the central part of town. This road actually covers over the stream that flows through the town and debouches into the east bay. On the left are many small shops and offices besides the Hotel Hafnia.

Near the top of Áarvegur, on the right, is the Danish High Commissioner's Office (*Rigsombudsmandskontor*), built in 1880 of Faroese basalt in the style of a villa with a tower. The residence lies in a leafy old garden that dates back some 175 years to the time when the Faroes first came under direct Danish rule after the Treaty of Kiel. Below this garden is a small steep path, Laðabrekka, that leads up to a plaque to Niels R. Finsen, the Nobel prize-winner. He was born in Tórshavn and gained his award for his discovery of ultraviolet light therapy in medicine.

We now come to the central area called Vaglið where five roads intersect – a place where people assemble in front of the Parliament building (*Løgtingshúsið*) at Ólavsøka. This timber-framed, turf-roofed building was erected in 1856 when the Trade Monopoly was abolished, but it was extended after the 1906 elections to make room for the increased number of members. It stands above a grassy slope where athletes parade, choirs sing national songs and speeches are made on the National Day, 29 July. On the green near Vaglið is a bronze bust of the poet R. C. Effersøe (1857–1916). Opposite the Parliament building is the famous Jacobsen's bookshop behind a row of trees on Vaglið. Originally a secondary school, erected in 1860, it has been a bookshop since 1918. On the other side of Mylnugøta, nearby, is a drab grey stone building put up in 1894 as the Town School, now the Town Hall.

Going north from Vaglið is the main, semi-pedestrianized street, named Niels Finsens gøta, after the town's most illustrious son. To the left, in a small square, is the Faroese Post Office. On the other side of the road is the Savings Bank (*Sparikassin*), in whose gardens is a fine bronze sculpture of a man and a woman by Janus Kamban, from 1972. In the middle of the street is a stainless steel creation called *Dancing children*, where flat outlines of boys and girls encircle a well, made by Fridtjof Joensen, 1984.

Further along we have the Faroese Bank (*Føroya Banki*) to the left, almost facing the Ebenezer Church. This large concrete building was erected in the 1960s for the use of the Plymouth Brethren congregation and has two meeting halls that can hold 500 and 1,200 people. The sect was founded here in 1865 by the Scottish missionary William Sloan, and has a large following in Tórshavn and Klaksvík, with about some 5,000 members. Adjoining the church is a brash new supermarket, so God and Mammon are very close to each other in the Faroes.

To the north of Vaglið, and standing above R. C. Effersøes gøta, is a basalt obelisk commemorating the visit of the Danish king Christian IX in 1874. The entrance is on the other side from Hoyvíksvegur. Where the two roads R. C. Effersøes gøta and Hoyvíksvegur cross on a rise, lower down, the first road changes its name to Jónas Broncks gøta (Jónas Bronck was born in Tórshavn and died in New York in 1643. He was supposed to have been the first settler in the Bronx.) On the other side is an open space with two small bronze figures by Eyvind Dalsgarð of a Faroese man carrying a creel (*leypur*) of peat and a woman with a milk-pail trudging along.

Up R. C. Effersøes gøta lies a large modern shopping centre, SMS (*Sólmiðstøðin*). This is also where the only dispensing chemist is located, while the telegraph station is also nearby.

The north-western part

One of the glories of Tórshavn was its plantation, *Viðarlund*, that lies north of the centre. It was started in the 1880s but did not really flourish until 1903, and contains many larches, firs and pines as well as other trees. The pleasant walks through shady lanes are open to the public. Unfortunately, the trees were devastated by two hurricanes in 1988–9 and a century's growth was undone in just a few days. In the centre of the plantation is a memorial to those who lost their lives during the last war. The bronze figure of a fisherman was made by the Norwegian sculptor Kåre Orud in 1956.

Mariukirkjan, the new Catholic church, was designed by a Faroese architect Árni Winther and was consecrated in 1987, replacing the uninspiring shed-like church that was erected in 1943. It is situated in Mariugøta, just below the plantation. The church is a functional, but charming building made out of basalt with a slanting copper roof and a round tower. Inside the rather small, informal church is a copy by a local Faroese craftsman of a wooden relief of the Virgin Mary from 1420 now in the National Museum in Copenhagen, intended for the Magnus cathedral in Kirkjubøur.

Listaskálin, the art gallery, is situated on the northern edge of the plantation, opposite the sports stadium. Here, they have a permanent collection of paintings by the most famous Faroese artists, Heinesen, Mykines, av Reyni and Smith, besides sculptures by Joensen and Kamban. Regular exhibitions are held here in the summer.

Beyond the sports complex, up on the northern ring

road, is the imaginative and exciting Nordic House (*Norðurlandshúsið*) opened in 1983 as a centre for promoting Nordic culture. It has a large hall that is used for concerts, plays and exhibitions, besides a lecture theatre.

Further along the ring road, you join R 10 and come to Hotel Borg, nestling in the hillside above Tórshavn. This interesting modern wooden-and-concrete construction has a turf roof and south-facing windows that give an excellent, commanding view over the town and the elongated outline of Nólsoy.

The south-western district

Behind the western bay is the real cultural centre of the town and there are interesting museums and libraries to visit.

Savnið 1940–5, the Faroe–British Museum, is on Doktora Jacobsens gøta to the east of the centre and opposite the old cemetery. It houses military uniforms and equipment, as well as photographs of daily life under the British occupation during the war.

Vesturkirkjan was built in 1975 and lies between Landave-gur and Mattalág, some 700 m south-west of the centre. There is no mistaking the triangular copper shape of this church that is so obvious when sailing into the harbour. The architectural appearance is utterly modern and quite out of sympathy with the Faroese landscape and tradition, but, once inside, your eye is carried ever-upward above the plain altar, giving a sense of infinite space. Even the organ, at the back of the church, is a little masterpiece of design. Unfortunately, the acoustics are very bad and the enormous roof continually leaks.

Føroyar Fornminnisavn, the Historical Museum, has two sections: archaeological and ethnological. They are both housed in the old stone-built National Library that lies above the new National Library in J. C. Svabos gøta, to the west of Vestaravág harbour. Downstairs is a permanent press-button display of the ecological food chain. There is a separate section on pilot whale hunting. Of special interest is the large-scale oceanographic model of the seabed around the Faroes. Up-stairs is a small display of various archaeological finds from excavations around the Faroes, mainly from Kvívík and Kirk-jubøur, and a display of the common tools and utensils used in the traditional farming society. Various objects of a religious nature are on display including plaster casts of the church stalls from Kirkjubøur, as well as a fourteenth-century wooden Madonna and Child from the same place.

Near the entrance path is a bas-relief of the inventor of the Faroese script, V. U. Hammershaimb made by the Faroese sculptor Janus Kamban in 1948.

Føroya Náttúrgripasavn and *Bátasavnið*, the Natural History Museum and Boat Museum, are both under one roof in a modern black wooden building in V. U. Hammershaimbs gøta. The Natural History Museum gives a comprehensive display of minerals, plants and animals. The collection of stuffed birds takes pride of place since this is the most varied family of animals found in the Faroes. The Boat Museum contains all the typical Faroese boats from the small rowing boat (*tríbekkur*) to a twelve-man boat (*seksæringur*). Also on display are boat-building tools, fishing equipment, and implements for seal and whale hunting, as well as fowling equipment.

Landsarkivet, the National Archives, lie lower down V. U. Hammershaimbs gøta. Its aim is to preserve all the official and private papers that can help explain how the society has changed over the years. It has a reading room for visiting scholars.

Fróðskaparsetur Føroya, the Faroese Academy, gives special university courses in Faroese language and literature, as well as in history and other subjects. The various institutions are in different parts of Tórshavn but the main buildings are opposite the Natural History Museum.

Landsbókasavn, the National Library, is in J. C. Svabos gøta. It is a copyright library and receives copies of all Faroese publications. Over 100,000 books are found here altogether and it is also possible to borrow books. Inside the library are busts of Dean J. Dahl and the writer H. A. Djurhuus.

An interesting piece of sculpture stands outside the Navigation School in J. C. Svabos gøta. It depicts a large golden hand lifting up a huge rock to reveal a small maiden. This is a memorial to the Faroese freebooter Nólsoyar-Páll (1766 –1809) and was presented to the Faroes by Iceland in 1973, almost a century after Iceland had obtained partial independence from Denmark. The moral was that Nólsoyar-

Páll had helped the Faroes to achieve a similar status and so it was fitting it should be placed outside the Navigation School that trained future skippers.

South of the white high-rise blocks of the hospital that stand up like square-bandaged, sore thumbs at the southern end of the town and dominate the view as one sails into harbour is the delightful old vicarage of Sandágerði. It lies off Dr Dahls gøta, just before crossing the bridge over the river, where a path to the left leads to the vicarage built in 1798. It has been restored and has reddish wooden walls and a turf roof with a pleasant garden full of flowering currants, as well as a few trees behind the encircling wall. This is a listed building but has not been used as a vicarage since the death of Dean Dahl in 1944. The place-name is appropriate as there are large grey sandbanks, where the river meets the sea.

Argir

The village of Argir is contiguous with Tórshavn but is separated from it by the river Sandá and the valley it has formed beneath Kirkjubøreyn (350 m) to the south. Argir has a sizeable population of 1,460 and it is the seventh largest place in the Faroes. It has no special industries and is simply a cheaper place to live in than Tórshavn because the local income tax is so much less. There is a fish factory and a marina behind the mole that protects the small harbour. The church is made of prefabricated concrete slabs with a corrugated iron roof and could be mistaken for anything but a church, except for the separate bell tower.

A track goes south of the village and leads to a large quarry that is painfully visible as you sail past the southern part of Streymoy.

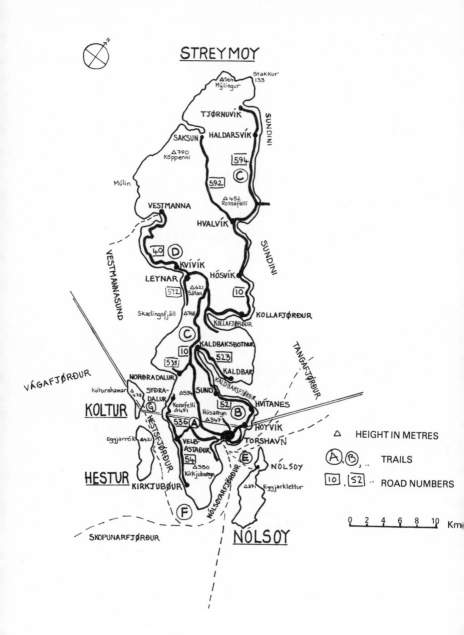

14   Streymoy, Nólsoy, Hestur and Koltur

Streymoy

'*Stream Island*' is the largest of all the islands; it measures 373.47 sq. km and contains 20,000 people – 42 per cent of the total population. The capital, Tórshavn, is in the south-east of the island with 16,000 inhabitants. Indeed, 80 per cent of the whole population live within a 25-km radius of Tórshavn. Streymoy is 47 km from south-east to north-west and 15 km from east to west. It is divided from Eysteroy by Sundini, through which only small boats can pass because of the many skerries, though now a bridge connects them. The east coast is punctuated by a number of bays and two deep fjords: Kollarfjørður and Kalbaksfjørður. On the west coast there are just the two bays of Saksun and Vestmanna. From Saksun to Hvalvík stretches a 10-km long valley that, in time, could eventually split the island in two. The northern end of the island finishes with the 133-m high stack, Stakkur. Along the western coast, from Mylingur (564 m) in the north to Múlin (303 m) in the south above Vestmanna, are some impressive bird-cliffs, steep and nearly vertical cliffs that are the favourite haunt of nesting birds. The highest peak is Koppenni (790 m) just below Saksun, but Skælingsfjall (768 m), to the north-west of Tórshavn, was once believed to be the highest mountain in the Faroes. A most spectacular waterfall called Fossá falls into Sundini below Haldarsvík. The largest natural lake is Leynavatn, but there are also larger water reservoirs above Vestmanna.

TRAIL A: TÓRSHAVN TO SYÐRADALUR

Velbastaður

We leave Tórshavn in a westerly direction along R(oute) 54, past the colourful, modern, prefabricated timber houses at the edge of the town. We then cross the river Sandá and climb up the rocky side of Tvørfelli (273 m) and across the stony ridge, full of tarns, until we come in sight of the two islands of Hestur and Koltur rising sharply out of the sea, across the fast-flowing sound. At this point the road descends in a series of bends to a point just above the small village of Velbastaður, where the road divides. R 54 continues left to Kirkjubøur while R 532 takes you to Velbastaður and from there R 536 goes on to Syðradalur.

The pleasing village of Velbastaður (population 100) stretches out above the shore, consisting of several hamlets made up of a mixture of old and new houses, a surprising number having the traditional turf roof. Such a uniformity in roofing is an interesting reflection on the local pride of place. This little farming community lies below the steep slopes of the mountain range.

Kirkjubøur

You can either take R 54 direct to Kirkjubøur or take a diversion through Velbastaður on R 532, to rejoin R 54 later. The road follows the lower contours of the mountainside, well above the shore. From here, the village of Skopun on Sandoy can be seen immediately opposite, as well as the projecting headland of Skálahøvdi, near the village of Skálavík on Sandoy's north-eastern shore.

On the shore below the steeply descending rocky mountainside of Kirkjubøreyn we get a superb sight of the old black Crown-farm building of Kirkjubøur (population 70), the ancient white church and the grey ruins of the cathedral. More incongruously, a large greenhouse for cultivating house plants is there to rival the cathedral in size. To park, take the left-hand road above the small village, since you will not find much space down by the shore.

Kirkjubøur is one of the most important historical sites in the whole of the Faroes, as well as being visually impressive, and is an absolute must for visitors. It was the ecclesiastical and cultural centre of the Faroes in the Middle Ages and came under the Norwegian Catholic archbishopric, which appointed the local bishop. One of these bishops, Erlend (1269–1308) started to build the cathedral, but he ran out of funds as well as popularity and the building was never completed. The nearby Crown-farm building is partly built on the site of the bishop's palace. The little white parish church is the oldest medieval church still in use in the Faroes. These three particular buildings are well worth a visit because of their uniqueness in the history of the Faroes.

This farmhouse has been the home of Crown-farmers here for centuries who also happen to have the largest farm in the whole of the Faroes. The part of the building nearest the shore is a different shape and at right-angles to the rest; it is also a private dwelling but has a kiosk in the basement where you can get tickets for the museum next door. The large log-framed north-eastern building was that part which was built on to the old bishop's palace and contains a huge living room (*roykstova*) that may be visited. The interior is impressive when you compare it with other Crown-farmhouses that have been turned into folk museums. This black-timbered building with a turf roof is enlivened by red windows and doors. It was here that the famous Faroese politician and author Jóannes Patursson was born in 1860. He is buried in the nearby churchyard.

The white-walled and lead-roofed church dates from AD 1111, and was very probably dedicated to the Virgin Mary. Such an extremely old building has obviously been restored many times, the last occasion being in 1967. Excavations have revealed the graves of possibly two bishops under the choir, one with a crozier: these are dated to *c.* 1260. The church served as a cathedral until the Reformation and it was during this period that the church acquired some superbly carved wooden stalls from Erik of Pomerania's time (1385–1459). These stalls were sold in 1874 and are now in the National Museum in Copenhagen, though plaster casts are to be found in the Historical Museum in Tórshavn. There is a fine altar piece by the Faroese artist S. Joensen-Mykines.

Not much is to be seen in the Magnus cathedral itself except for the architecture of its looming, grey walls and the consecration crosses. It is 26.5 by 10.75 m externally and just 9 m high. On the external eastern wall is a soapstone carving of the crucifixion, behind which relics were found, supposedly those of St Magnus. Magnus was Earl of Orkney and he was murdered there by Earl Håkon of Norway in AD 1116. Currently, ambitious plans are being made to restore or even complete the cathedral at Kirkjubøur.

Up the green hillside, above the cathedral, is Sverre's cave, where king Sverre (1184–1202) was supposed to have been born. He was, allegedly, educated in Kirkjubøur before he ascended the throne in Norway.

A hundred metres east of the cathedral are the remains of what might have been the first church here, but most of it has been washed into the sea and only a small building that served as a mortuary is now left.

Syðradalur

Going past Velbastaður along R 536, the road climbs up the sides of Steinafjall (416 m) and Konufelli (491 m) with a steep rockface on one side and a precipitous drop on the other. Eventually after 8 km we reach Syðradalur, but not before a sharp, winding descent down to this small hamlet of one farm and a couple of houses. It has an attractive waterfall and a fine view over to Koltur and Vágar.

Although it is only a couple of kilometres south of Norðradalur, no direct road connection exists for the way is blocked by the steep sides of Tunguliðfjall (561 m). Thus, we have to return to Tórshavn.

TRAIL B: TÓRSHAVN TO KALDBAK

Hoyvík

Driving north along Hvítanesvegur (R 52) out of Tórshavn and past the Studentaskúli you take a small road, Kúrdals-vegur, to the right towards the former Agricultural Research Station at Hoyvík which are now the Archaeological Museum offices. Good views are to be had across the water to Nólsoy and to Sandoy, in the south.

Nearby is the steep cliff, Kyrberg, from where you get a panoramic view of Eysturoy and the mountain tops of Borðoy to the north, while below are the skerries of Hoyvíkshólmur, with a lighthouse warning of its dangers.

Hvítanes

Further along R 52 we come to the small village of Hvítanes, which lies further north, with only a dozen houses near to the rocky shore. At the end of the village road are a couple of derelict concrete boathouses above the cliffs, with a view beyond.

Sund

Before we come to the hamlet of Sund, along R 52, we pass by the incinerator plant for Tórshavn with its enormous tall blue chimney. From here we see across Tangafjørður to Toftir on Eysturoy, as well as to Kaldbak just across the water.

At Sund there is a large quay and a diesel power station together with a cluster of large oil tanks. Although difficult to spy, a small old farmhouse lies next to these modern installations.

Kaldbaksbotnur

R 52 is a new road and is cut into the steeply sloping hillside. Cascading waterfalls pour down from the rocky edges above, alongside the roadway.

Kaldbaksbotnur lies at the end of the fjord and at the head of a kettle-valley, with just a few farmhouses. It is planned to drive a tunnel from here to Signabøur on Kollafjørður to the north, in order to obviate going across the high mountainous range that is frequently fog-bound. From here the NATO building at Mjørkadalur, high up the mountainside, can just be seen.

Numerous fish farms are found in Kaldbaksfjørður where salmon, trout and mussels are cultivated. The fjord offers a sheltered area for wild fish and many people from Tórshavn take their little boats here for a spot of quiet evening fishing.

Kaldbak

The Kaldbak road (R 523) runs below steep cliffs and along the shore lined with fish farms. An impressive waterfall is passed before entering the village. Until recently, Kaldbak supplied Tórshavn with most of its milk and it had a regular, private milk-boat connection.

A black and white, wooden, turf-roofed church with a white spire was built way back in 1835 and is an excellent example of the early nineteenth-century Faroese churches. It has an intricately carved wooden screen. Inside the altar rail the floor is covered with sheepskins.

A number of separate hamlets make up this pleasant village of Kaldbak with its mixture of old and modern housing. Its former relative isolation has enabled it to maintain a number of the traditional features: old houses, green infields and a stone boundary wall. Amusingly enough, a plastic-boat factory here produces moulded boats that are direct copies of the traditional, wooden clinker-built Faroese boats.

TRAIL C: TÓRSHAVN TO TJØRNUVÍK

Norðradalur

About 9 km north of Tórshavn, along R 10, and just past Stidjafjall (546 m) a left-hand turn takes you to Norðradalur on R 538. This is a small serpentine road that winds steeply down the kettle-valley until the road forks. A couple of kilometres further on, to the right, is the lonely farmstead of Úti á Fløtum. Further out still, at Dalsnípa, is a smolt farm where young salmon are bred in large circular tanks. The stream from the mountain behind feeds the tanks with fresh water.

From Úti á Fløtum, Norðradalur can be seen on the other side of a large fissure, Dalagjógv, that causes the road to divide higher up. It is also possible to glimpse Syðradalur 3 km down the coast, beyond the large mountain, Tungulíðfjall (501 m), that separates it from Norðradalur. Here we have clear views of Koltur and Hestur to the south.

Returning to the road junction, Norðradalur lies to the right and consists of three houses with outbuildings, nestling in a cirque-like valley. Here, too, we find a fish-breeding plant at the foot of a waterfall.

Taking R 10 out of Tórshavn, by way of Oyggjarvegur, you go past Norðurlandahúsið and climb up past Hotel Borg on the left. From here an excellent panoramic view is obtained over the whole of Tórshavn and out over Nólsoy. Eventually, reaching 300 m up the mountain Húsareyn, you continue over the mountains, most likely shrouded in clouds. Passing the road to Norðradalur to the left you then, at Mjørkadalur, swing past the NATO control centre and living quarters. This is a well-designed but also well-camouflaged building with a turf roof, nestling in the side of the mountain, overlooking Kaldbaksfjørður. A little further on is a twisty road to the left up to Sornfelli (749 m) where the NATO tropospheric transmitters are placed, conveying messages from Keflavík in Iceland to Fylingdales in Yorkshire. This station has no other military purpose than information transmission. Just before coming to the restricted military area it is possible, on a clear day, to get a bird's eye view of both the northern and southern islands of the Faroes.

The mountainous R 10 road is 20 km long but at an average height of 300 m it affords occasional spectacular views of the fjords and islands below. Eventually, the road descends sharply to meet R 40 to Vestmanna. A petrol station is found here at this junction as well as a cafeteria. The right-hand fork is R 10, continuing to Kollafjørður.

Kollafjørður

At the head of the fjord there is a cultivated area on the right called Oyrareingir and, further along, the hamlet of Signabøur. In the mountainside you can see the opening of the tunnel that will eventually lead to Kaldbaksbotnur. Only a narrow, cultivated strip of land lies near the road that runs along the shore. Because of the steeply sloping sides of the fjord, this restriction on available land may account for the fact that Kollafjørður village stretches 7 km along this fjord, making it the longest village in the Faroes. In fact, this densely populated section (870 people) is composed of many small hamlets that are grouped under a single local authority or *kommune*. It was once a *ting*-place, where assemblies were held in the olden days.

An upper by-pass road skirts the first half of the village which lies close to the shore. In the middle is a traditional small black and white timbered church built in 1837. Some older houses are found just here, as well as a waterfall. At this point, the by-pass road now continues close to the shore while the old road is higher up, but they join up later at the point of Kjalnes, at the mouth of Sundini – the sound that flows between Streymoy and Eysturoy. A number of fish farms line this fjord.

Fish farming is a new development and many villagers are

Fámjin: This small village is unusual in being on the western coast and it can be seen to lie beneath a large mountain, Knúkin. See Chapter 19.

Landscape

Víðareiði: Under this enormous cirque, lies this small village. See Chapter 16.

Feeding sheep: Sheep have to be fed in the winter from the hay that has been garnered from the fields. [Note their different colours.]

Húsavík: This is the site of the Lady of Húsavík's residence. The walls in the foreground are their remains. This is an old part of the village. See Chapter 18.

Gjógv: The old black houses with corrugated-iron roofs form a perfect setting beneath the triangular mountain-top of Middagsfjall. The division of the infield is clearly seen. See Chapter 15.

Tórshavn: This is a very colourful view of the warehouses in Vesturavág, surmounted by a glimpse of the old church. Today, the marina is more organized.

Tinganes: Such a view greets you when you enter Tórshavn harbour. Details of these old buildings is given in Chapter 13.

turning to this in order to increase their incomes, because the salmon, trout and mussels, so-raised, find a ready market in the lucrative export trade.

Hósvík

R 10 continues from Kollafjørður, round the steep cliffs along Sundini. Interesting views are now to be had across the sound to the hamlet of Morskranes and the village of Selatrað. The village of Hósvík (population 270) lies around a small attrac-   *270* tive bay that contains a water-meadow at its head with some old-fashioned boathouses on the road beside it. The church is made of white concrete and begun in 1927 but it looks rather like a cross between a transformer station and an ordinary house with a tiled roof. A couple of nice waterfalls stream down the mountainsides. This was once the ferry terminal for Selatrað on Eysturoy, before the bridge connecting the two islands was built.

Hvalvík

As we leave Hósvík, the sound begins to narrow and the opposite shore appears so steep that no road could ever be possibly be built along its slopes. As we go north, Oyri village comes into view, on the other side. We pass by við Air, which was an old whaling station but is now the site of a new rehabilitation centre. However, the rusty old works still remain.

Hvalvík (population 370) lies on the west side of a broad   *370* bay, bisected by the river Stórá, while on the other side is the small hamlet of Streymnes. As the name suggests, this is a good place for catching the pilot whale.

One of the oldest preserved traditional wooden churches is situated in the middle of the village, on the road to Saksun. The previous church was built in 1700 but was destroyed by a storm in 1829. A new church was built immediately, with Pomeranian pine from a ship that had been stranded the previous year in Saksun. It has black wooden walls a turf roof and a white tower. The inside of the church is unpainted but it has a remarkable painted pulpit that dates back to 1609 and originally stood in Tórshavn. The pulpit bears sabre marks, deriving from a pirate raid in 1677, when the Tórshavn church was plundered.

Near the church is a small plantation – a rare sight in the Faroes. Also, close by, are some old houses with turf or corrugated iron roofs. The village has quite a large, unspoiled infield. Many infields have been recently rationalized, the land is divided up by wire fences and the fields contain sheep or new houses, built in the middle. Whether or not the infield has been rationalized tells you where the villagers place their main priorities.

Streymnes lies across the broad river flowing over wide, flat rocks. The straggle of oldish houses that form most of this hamlet is at the bottom slopes of Rossafelli (448 m). Streams often act as dividing lines between rival factions of a single village, who oppose each other for a variety of reasons.

Saksun

R 592 from Hvalvík leads through a 10-km long valley to the small hamlet of Saksun (population 26), on the west side of Streymoy. First, you pass along the broad river Stórá, flowing shallowly over horizontal rocks, outside Hvalvík. The valley narrows and, after the watershed, we come to a small lake, Saksunarvatn, that is good for salmon and trout fishing. Crossing the river Dalsá, we pass some modern summerhouses on the left, as well as a number of waterfalls streaming off the steep mountainsides.

Saksun church (brought here from Tjørnuvík) stands to the left, by itself, some 50 m above the silted-up round bay called Pollur. The sand barrier was formed during a dreadful storm several centuries ago, but before then it was a good harbour. As related earlier, a timber cargo boat was stranded here in 1828 as it sought shelter, and the cargo of 800 planks of pine was used to build many houses, as well as Hvalvík church.

Saksun's attraction, apart from its idyllic position and spectacular views, is the folk museum: *Dúvugarður*. This is an old Crown-farm building that was lived in up to the 1940s. The museum has a boulder foundation, tarred wooden walls and a turf roof. Both the outside and inside are representative of a typical but comparatively rich, farmhouse. The oldest part is some three centuries old but many additions have been

made over the years. The earthen floor has been made solid
with concrete but the scrubbed pine walls are intact. The
roykstova or work-room contains all the usual things one
expects to find: wooden utensils, spinning wheels, milk
churns, carrying baskets and of course a fireplace and a lum or
opening in the roof to let the smoke out, now covered by glass.
It has box beds and a parlour (*glasstova*) where the minister
would stay when he came to hold services. At one time up to 20
people lived in this one small house!

A few miles north of Hvalvík we come to the bridge over
Sundini that links Streymoy and Eysturoy. The bridge (Sundalagsbrúgvin) was finished in 1976 and is 226 m long; it is the
only bridge in the Faroes. On both shores are many fish farms;
some are large permanent concrete pens, while scores of
ring-nets for growing salmon and trout dot the sound with
their bright colours.

Going north, the road changes its number to R 594 after the
bridge. It runs along the shore past two small hamlets – Nesvík
and Langasandur, whose main industry is fish farming.
Dozens of ring-nets with bright blue plastic tubing supporting
the cage-nets are surrounded by many brilliant red buoys and
make a colourful sight, in comparison with the dull grey
concrete fish-tanks, nearby.

A little further on we climb up the hillside and come to an
impressive waterfall at Fossdalur which cascades 140 m down
a deep cleft in the mountainside. From here, we see across to
the high mountain ranges on Eysturoy and the highest mountain in the Faroes, Slættaratindur (882 m) which, surprisingly,
is flat on top and should not be confused with the nearby
triangular peak of Vaðhorn (726 m).

Haldarsvík

Haldarsvík (population 220) lies around a small bay, protected by a breakwater, and is a very neat and compact village
under the sloping green mountainside. However, down near
the quay are many neglected wooden sheds with brown, rusty,
corrugated iron roofs which contrast with the well-kept dwelling houses in the centre and the modern fish processing plant
near the harbour. It has a most unusual white octagonal stone
church which was built as early as 1856 – the year of the

abolition of the Royal Monopoly. The design is probably based on Fredriksberg church in Copenhagen. An attractive waterfall can be seen from the church which lies on the far side of the stream from the village proper. Above the church, a memorial in metal has been erected to those lost at sea. It is a futuristic piece made by the Faroese sculptor Janus Kamban, consisting of three hoops of aluminium, enclosing a large silver coloured ball.

Tjørnuvík

From Haldarsvík, the road swings round, bringing the village of Eiði on the other side of the sound into full view. As the name suggests, this village is built on an isthmus. Since the houses are built up the slope of the hill you can see most of the village, as well as the prominent white church on the very isthmus itself.

Climbing upwards, the road goes around Hægstafjall (469 m) where a steep descent takes you into Tjørnuvík (population 75). Because of its sheltered position, facing north-east, the sun does not shine on this picturesque village for more than a third of the year.

The white wooden church has a red corrugated roof and was built in 1936. The old church was moved to Saksun in 1858 after the Haldarsvík church was built.

Numerous waterfalls pour their water down the steep cliffs, cutting deep clefts in the process and forming small streams at the bottom that meander through the infield to the grey sandy beach. On the northern side is a landing-stage next to a narrow deep fissure, or *gjógv*, that is only a rowing boat's width across and about 10 m deep. A windlass is used to haul the boats up from the clear seawater below. From this vantage point, at the edge of the bay, you have an excellent vista of the almost vertical cliffs of Kollur (343 m) that lie beyond Eiði at the tip of Eysturoy. Standing in the sea, in front of those cliffs, are the two large stacks *Risin and Kellingin* – the Giant and the Hag.

In 1956 a dozen Viking graves were found in Tjørnuvík. They were situated near the bend in the road, before crossing the river, coming into the village. A Celtic brooch was among the finds, which can be seen in the Historical Museum in Tórshavn, near Fróðskaparsetur.

Pollen-analysis has shown that a significant change in

vegetation took place here in the eighth century AD, suggesting that people were living here, though no supporting archaeological evidence has been found. The speculation is that Irish hermits might have been here, but this is probably wishful thinking.

TRAIL D: TÓRSHAVN TO VESTMANNA

The following villages are situated along R 40 to Vestmanna, after the petrol station junction with R 10 that goes to Kollafjørður.

Leynar

From the petrol station outside Kollafjørður the road divides, and R 10 goes right to Sundini and on to Leirvík, while R 40 goes to Vestmanna. Soon you pass a lake, Mjauvøtn, and then through a 800-m tunnel (completed in 1977) to the end of Leynarvatn. Both lakes are good fishing places and licences can be obtained at the petrol station. In 1973 a salmon ladder was built from Vestmannasund to help the fish up the river Leynará.

Leynar village (population 85) lies to the left of R 40, along R 572. The river Leynará runs out onto a golden beach by the shore. From here you can see across the sound to the east coast of Vágar. Leynar is a straggly village struggling up the hillside, with some old houses but also with many large modern houses – it is a kind of rural suburb of Tórshavn.

R 572 continues along the side of the mountain Sátan (621 m), meaning 'haystack', to the small hamlet of Skælingur which has only half a dozen houses. This is a lovely situation but it has no access to the sea because the cliffsides fall directly into the water. From the road end you can see Kvívík to the north. An old track leads 8 km southwards over the hills to Úti á Fløtum, near Norðradalur. Tracks such as this were once marked by a series of cairns but many have fallen into disuse. You should exercise the greatest caution if you attempt to walk these paths.

Kvívík

After passing Leynar on R 40, the road swings along the coast of Vestmannasund and through the small hamlet of Stykkið before rising up the mountainside to by-pass Kvívík. A small road to the left leads down into the village itself, with a population of 350.

Kvívík is charmingly situated on a bay at the end of a steep-sided valley through which flows a large river, appropriately named Stórá – 'stór' meaning large and 'á' river. The white stone church with a slate roof has, on the church door, a relief of a crown above the letters C IX and the date 1903. This denotes the reign of King Christian IX of Denmark and when the church was built. Nearby is the old vicarage with a turf roof – both attractive buildings.

Down near the shore, two Viking buildings were excavated in 1942 after they had been discovered by somebody who wished to extend his own house. The larger one was some 21 m long and 5.75 m wide and consisted of a single room with a central fireplace. The other building, alongside, was the byre, which could have held a dozen cows. Both structures were built along a north–south axis but the southern parts have been washed away by the sea. The finds were typical of the twelfth century and are now in the Tórshavn Historical Museum.

Vestmanna

R 40 from Kvívík wriggles its way around the mountainsides, high above Vestmanna sound, overlooking the neighbouring island of Vágar. Eventually the road swings round and down to Vestmanna bay around which 1,300 inhabitants live. As we descend, we first come to the small village of Válur, which technically belongs to Kvívík parish but is functionally part of Vestmanna, the largest village on Streymoy.

Vestmanna's growth can partly be attributed to its excellent natural harbour. It is also the ferry terminal for Vágar and its airport. Behind the village are several lakes and reservoirs, used for hydro-electricity generation. Huge pipes spring out of the mountainside feeding several power stations around the bay.

Colourful houses are arrayed in layers up the lower slopes from the waterfront. The white stone church (1895) is in the western part of the village, where there is also a monument to

those lost at sea – a statue of a man holding a spear, made by
Janus Kamban in 1962.

Nólsoy

'Needle Island', or Nólsoy, is 10.28 sq. km in area and has a
village of the same name. It is 9 km from north-west to
south-east and just 2 km wide. It is separated from Tórshavn,
5 km away, by Nólsoyarfjørður. The village is on an isthmus
that divides the island in two. At one time the village was on
the other side of the isthmus, but this site was abandoned
because of its exposed position. It is said that the island
received its name because it has a sharp pointed end. This
northern end of the island is relatively low lying, being only
74 m high, but the coast itself is steep and vertical in places.
The village lies just north of the isthmus that separates the 'tip'
of the needle from the massive, humped mass of the larger,
southern end which is complete with an 'eye' – Borðholið, a
hole through the cliffs, through which you can sail. The highest
point is Eggjaklettur (371 m) but the southern part ends with a
slope containing lakes and a lighthouse at the very end. The
eastern side has steep bird-cliffs. What is clearly visible, from
the sea, are the various banded layers of basalt that make up
the southern part of Nólsoy.

TRAIL E: TÓRSHAVN TO NÓLSOY

The island and the small colourful village of Nólsoy lie in full
sight of Tórshavn and it takes only twenty minutes to get there
by the little ferryboat *Ritan* (the *Kittiwake*), which leaves from
the terminal in Tórshavn harbour. Halfway across
Nólsoyfjørður, you get an excellent panorama of Tórshavn,
from Argir in the south to Hoyvík in the north. The town is
spread out before you, as it extends up the broad valley
between Húsareyn (347 m) on the right and Kirkjubøreyn
(350 m) on the left. Looking north, the brightly coloured
houses of Strendur and Toftir, on either side of Skálafjørður,
can be seen. Sandoy can also be made out to the south.

As you approach Nólsoy (population 320), its apparent
prettiness dissolves. Facing the quayside is a semicircle of grey,
concrete boathouses, each with concrete landing slips, no

longer in use. Even the old church (1863), white and grey near the quay, is uninspiring. Only the modern houses on the outskirts are cheerfully coloured.

To the south of the harbour is a new quay and a fish factory, while perched on the rocks around the harbour are large numbers of herring gulls and black-backed gulls who, periodically, swoop onto the quayside to snatch up any fish offal that is lying around.

You enter the village through an arch of whalebones. Like many Faroese villages, it is heavily nucleated, with the houses all grouped very close together and staggered in parallel rows up the hillside, overlooking the harbour. Most of the houses are from earlier this century and look it.

It is possible to walk along a path up to the northern tip of the island, covered in grass since it is the infield. Various wild flowers like buttercups, daisies, campion and white clover are found, as elsewhere. The infield has been rationalized and is divided up by wire fences. Overhead, oystercatchers wheel and call during the summer.

At the end of the northern point, the cliffs fall vertically more than 30 m down to the sea, where dislodged basalt boulders have been rounded by the waves. From this vantage point, you can see the many neat, black and white ferries passing on their separate journeys up and down between the islands. Besides looking across to Tórshavn, it is possible to get an uninterrupted view up Tangafjørður towards Selatrað on Eysturoy, as well as to Nes and the various peninsulas of Eysturoy and Borðoy to the north. There is always a sense of closeness as you look around.

Returning towards the village, a small path to the left winds up the hill above the village and gives a unique sight of the eastern side of Nólsoy, with its nearly vertical cliffs.

Down by the harbour, a taxidermist's shop sells all sorts of stuffed birds, both local and exotic. These souvenirs can also be purchased in the many gift shops in the islands. The most common bird on offer is, of course, the puffin, caught by the thousand as they are a local delicacy. They are sold to the restaurants and shops for a couple of pounds each. Considering that, on a good day, a fowler can catch 500 birds, this is a good, tax-free source of income in the season. However, it is a dangerous and risky business to climb down the bird-cliffs.

A path also goes across the mountainous southern part of the island, some 7 km in length, to the manned lighthouse at Kapulin. Cairns line this path but it is always subject to sudden fog and mist, when it is easy to lose one's way.

Hestur

This small island, known as 'The Horse' is only 6.09 sq. km in area and is separated from Streymoy by Hestsfjørður, from Koltur by Koltursund and from Sandoy by Skopunarfjørður. Sixty people live in the village on the sloping north-east side of the island. The west side has steep bird-cliffs that plunge into the sea, where there are many stacks. The highest point is Eyggarók (421 m) in the north whence the high flat land slopes southwards towards several lakes.

TRAILS F AND G: TÓRSHAVN TO HESTUR AND KOLTUR

Ritan will take you to both these islands from Tórshavn. As only one family lives on Koltur, the boat calls there only on request, but there is also a separate helicopter service to Koltur. The boat takes an hour to Hestur and another half hour to Koltur. Although the names of these two islands are popularly taken to mean 'Horse' and 'Colt', there is some doubt if these derivations are etymologically sound.

When sailing along the southern edge of Streymoy you get a grand sight of the long high ridge of Nólsoy, with its layers of striated basalt. The boat hugs the rocky coast and passes the deserted farm at Uti á Bø at the southern tip of Streymoy, on the right. We then come quite close to the small attractive village of Kirkjubøur and can see how it lies under the sloping mountainside, from where there are occasional rockfalls. Also visible is the large quarry next to the village which has been used to get stone for a new harbour on Hestur, since they have no suitable stone.

Crossing the fast flowing waters of Hestfjørður, we see the towering dome of Kolturshamar (478 m) rising directly out of the sea to the north-west. The mountains on Hestur are not that much lower – Múlin and Eggjarrok are both 421 m – but they form a ridge and it is below these green slopes that the small colourful village of Hestur (population 60) lies by the shore, in the middle of the island.

Coming along the southern coast of Hestur, emerald patches of grass show up along the steeply sloping infield. The village is tightly built and has some 25 houses and a white stone church with a red roof, built in 1910. The quayside is small and is being extended to make it safer. At the southern tip of the island is an unmanned lighthouse that can be seen *en route* to Sandoy.

Koltur

'The Colt' is the island companion of Hestur from which it is separated by Koltursund. It is just 2.45 sq. km in area and only one family lives there. A high peak, Kolturshamar (478 m), lies to the north but the ground quickly slopes to a small, flat area where the hamlet is to be found. The west side also has steep bird-cliffs.

Going on to Koltur, you pass the long green outfield of Hestur under its boundary wall. The village of Velbastaður is seen across the fjord. The southern end of Koltur is only 100 m high and the hamlet of Koltur is on the lowest part of the island with just a small sandy beach and a couple of houses. Parts of the farm are several hundred years old and these buildings are now protected as national monuments.

The position of Koltur hamlet makes it exposed to winter storms and large breakers have often torn away buildings. A helipad is there for regular journeys as well as for emergencies. The rugged coast of Streymoy can be seen opposite with some of the small hamlets there.

EYSTUROY

Risin
Kellingin
△343 Kollur
EIÐI
SUNDINI
662/632
LJÓSÁ
△882 Slættaratindur
GJÓGV
DJÚPINI
△601 Middagsfjäll
△726 Vaðhorn
FUNNINGUR
62
H
△697
FUNNINGSFJØRÐUR
662
SVÍNÁIR
634
ELDUVÍK
NORDSKÁLI
△721 Hægstafjäll
OYNDARFJØRÐUR
10
692
I
OYNDARFJØRÐUR
SUNDINI
OYRI
△788 Múlatindur
△731 Blábjørg
△626
HELLUR
FUGLAFJØRÐUR
△627 Húsafelli
10/645
LEIRVÍKSFJØRÐUR
65
SKÁLAFJØRÐUR
NORÐRAGØTA
FUGLAFJØRÐUR
SELATRAÐ
TANGAFJØRÐUR
J
SKÁLAFJØRÐUR
69
GØTUEIÐI
△347
L
70
LEIRVÍK
69
SKÁLI
10
GØTUGJÓGV
STØRUGØTA
△614 Sigatindur
MORSKRANES
K
SKIPANES
KOLBANARGJÓGV
SØLDAFJØRÐUR
LAMBAREIÐI
GØTUVÍK
INNAN SJÓGV
VIÐ SJÓGV
683
LAMBI
STRENDUR
10
GLYVRAR
RUNAVÍK
TOFTIR
10
SALTNES
NES
685
LAMBAVÍK
RITUVÍK
ÆÐUVÍK

0 1 2 3 4 5

15 Eysturoy

'Eastern Island' is not only the second largest in size with 286.33 sq. km, but it also has the largest number of villages of any island in the Faroes: 35, with a total population of 10,500. From south-east to north-west it is 35 km while the greatest width is 18 km. It is separated in the west from Streymoy by the narrow straits of Sundini (over which there is a bridge) and in the east from Kalsoy and Borðoy by Djúpini and Leirvíksfjørður. The east coast is especially indented with fjords: from north to south, they are Funningsfjørður, Oyndnarfjørður, Fuglafjørður, Gøtuvík and Lambavík. From the south-west the 12-km long Skálafjørður runs north-east, part of which is called Kongshavn (King's harbour) because it is a safe refuge. Some 6 km separate the ends of Skálafjørður and Funningsfjørður, with only a 80-m high valley between them that effectively divides the island in two distinct halves, geographically speaking, and isolated the villages before roads were built.

Slættaratindur (882 m), meaning 'flat on top', is in the north and is the highest mountain in the Faroes. At the northern tip of the island, near the village of Eiði, are the two renowned stacks: *Risin and Kellingin*.

The shores of Skálafjørður are the most densely populated part of the island from Runavík in the east, to Skáli and

Strendur on the other side. Other important villages are Fuglafjørður, Leirvík and Gøta on the east coast and Eiði on the north-west coast. Tórshavn can now be reached by road through a 2.5-km tunnel and a bridge over Sundini.

TRAIL H: SUNDALAGSBRÚGVIN TO ELDUVÍK

Oyri

Crossing the bridge at Sundini, you turn right at the petrol station onto R 692 for Oyri. The hamlet of Oyrabakki here grew up after the bridge was opened in 1976. A huge concrete fish farm is nearby. A sprinkling of houses line the road towards the compact village of Oyri where the road stops at a large fish factory. Oyri has no church yet the population is about 200.

Three roads fan out at the Eysturoy end of the bridge: R 692 on the right for Oyri, R 10 that climbs up the hill and through a tunnel towards Leirvík and R 62 on the left that goes to Eiði along the sound.

North of the bridge we come first to Norðskáli, situated on a flat stretch by the sound. It has a white concrete church with a black corrugated roof, built in 1932. After the bridge was erected, the church was doubled in length, as it now had to serve all the 500 villagers between Oyri and Eiði. The houses in this part of the village are from the early part of this century, in the usual mixture of colours. A couple of kilometres further on is the small hamlet of Svínáir. Just before this hamlet, where the river Svíná falls into the sound, is Gjánoyri where the first whaling station in the Faroes was built in 1894.

Driving further along the sound you have an excellent view of the imposing waterfall of Fossdalur opposite. It is also possible to glimpse Haldarsvík and Eiði to the north.

The next village is Ljósá with only 40 or so people. It lies down by the shore with a small circular harbour. The infield is now continuous along the coast. Just before we come to Eiði (population 700) we pass a waterfall and then a small road to the right leading up to Eiðisvatn, 155 m above sea-level. This lake is used for hydro-power but is also good for fishing. The next road to the right is R 662 to Funningur and Gjógv. We proceed, however, down R 62 to Eiði.

Eiði

As Eiði lies on an isthmus and the cliffs on this side are so steep, there is no proper bay, although it now has a large harbour, protected by two breakwaters. Most villages at the head of a natural bay are ranged around the shore, with the windows of the houses overlooking the bay. Eiði, contrariwise, is built around the lower slopes of a hill, Kollur (343 m), on the western side of the isthmus and so the houses along the southern road face the sound but those closer to the isthmus tend to be facing east.

The church stands almost alone in the middle of the isthmus and above the quay. It was erected in 1881 and is built in the Romantic style out of basalt. It is painted white and has a slate roof and a tower with a large copper dome. Faroese churches are generally built by the shore and often on the other side of the stream that bisects most villages, thus creating 'sacred' and 'profane' spheres, so to speak. Probably a simple explanation is that one should not build on the infield. However, the proximity of the church and its accompanying graveyard to both salt and fresh water might be symbolic of some kind of holy protection of these two life-sustaining elements. It has been said that the shoreline position of the church meant that it was the last thing you saw when going out to sea but the first thing to be seen when returning. That statement suggests the very sight of the church was a blessing when on the salt water.

The houses here are built in rows up the hillside, the oldest ones nearer the church. A road runs westwards and has many large new houses along it, after which a path continues over the infield towards the coast, from where you can see the road going to Tjørnuvík on Streymoy, on the other side.

In the village itself a road goes northwards over the isthmus to a beach that faces the Atlantic. It passes a small lake that has been cleaned and restocked with salmon. A pebble beach lines the shore and here you see the great, rocky promontories of north Eysturoy.

In the centre of the village are the older houses, as well as a quiet enclosure dedicated to those lost at sea. It has a bronze statue of a woman and child, while tablets all around record the dead. In the streets are some delightful rubbish bins, in the form of model houses, that enjoin you to keep the village clean.

Overlooking this engaging village is a large white hotel with superb vistas over the lake and sea as well as down the sound. A large fish factory and some boat sheds are situated down near the harbour.

From Eiði we climb back along R 662 and around the mountainside. On the bend we get a glimpse of *Risin and Kellingin* sticking out beyond the head of Kollur. Like many such unusual stacks, stories are attached to them that have a common theme. This story suggests that Iceland wanted to annex the Faroes and a giant and his wife were sent to pull the islands to Iceland. The giant stood in the sea while his wife climbed up to fix a rope for him to tow away the islands. On the first attempt, the giant tugged too hard and part of the cliff simply came away and fell into the sea where it still lies. On the second try, as the giant struggled in vain, his wife, at the top of the cliff, saw the sun beginning to rise and so she rushed down to warn her husband. But she was too late: the sun's rays turned them both to stone!

Going off to the right is a private road leading to the long-range navigation station (*Loran*) and its transmitter that were erected in 1959.

The road then bends back in a southerly direction as it twists and turns below the southern edge of the Faroes' highest mountain. Slættaratindur (882 m), and north of Vaðhorn (726 m). It passes by the large reservoir of Eiðisvatn with its two big dams. Because of the height of this reservoir you get the curious illusion, looking towards Haldarsvík, that there is an uninterrupted stretch of water from here to that village, apparently on the other side of a large lake!

Up the western slopes are green meadows and many cattle in the outfield. The pass is fairly narrow and contains several hairpin bends, but at the top is a stupendous scene in front, over Funningsfjørður, across to the high mountain peaks of the narrow island of Kalsoy with its steep, inhospitable western coastline.

Over the pass we have yet another hairpin bend to negotiate and, about one-third of the way down, the road divides: R 632 to the left goes to Gjógv while R 662 on the right snakes its way through many hairpin bends down to Funningur. From this vantage point (400 m high) we get a stunning sight of the small, compact village of Funningur, sandwiched between the lower end of the Middagsfjall (601 m) and Húsarfjall (697 m) to the south that falls sharply to the fjord. The mountains are very green and truly alpine meadows, while the horizontal basalt layers that make up the Faroes are clearly visible, interrupted by occasional lines of brown tuff.

Gjógv

At the junction of R 632 and R 662, we continue ahead for 5 km along R 632, and after another hairpin bend at Gjáarskarð (308 m), we enter a broad valley running between the mountains towards Gjógv (population 75). The infield stretches a long way up the valley but the small and beautiful village itself lies closely huddled together at the shore's edge.

The small church of white concrete with a green corrugated roof was begun in 1925 and notably consecrated in 1929 by Dean Dahl, with the first service ever to be held in Faroese. Nearby is a bronze memorial statue by Janus Kamban to those lost at sea, depicting a woman and her two young sons looking out to sea. It was unveiled in 1971.

Several old houses with tarred wooden sides and turf roofs stand in the middle of the village near the stream that flows through it. One of these houses is an old shop that is well worth looking into. From here you can see the pyramidical top of Middagsfjall (601 m) to the south. There is even a duck pond to complete this idyllic picture.

At the northern edge of the village is the 188-m long fissure that gives the village its name. It functions as a harbour, but only small boats can use it as it is quite narrow. A steep flight of steps leads up from the water to a windlass at the top for pulling the boats up, as it is unsafe to leave them down in the water. Above the water line on the rocks is bright green lichen, while in the grassy ledges of the cleft, puffins have their nests, deep inside the turf.

Some old boathouses lie near the shore, as well as a fish breeding farm. Around the village are several potato patches using the lazy-bed method of cultivation. You can see over the waters to the mountainous ridges on the neighbouring island of Kalsoy.

Funningur

From Gjógv we return up to the junction where R 662 begins its dizzying zigzag descent down the kettle-valley to Funningur and its 115 inhabitants. The river divides this pretty little village in two. The old black wooden-sided church has a turf roof and was built in 1847, near the water's edge, by the side of the river. The pews are of unpainted mahogany and it has a beautifully carved screen. In the tower is a small door that at one time was used to store the heavy ropes used for descending the bird-cliffs.

Boathouses are found by the quay as well as quite a number of drying-houses (*hjallur*) for fish and lamb. The sheep are supposed to be particularly fine here and make excellent dried lamb (*skjerpikjøt*).

R 662 continues past the village and along the shore of this very long fjord for 6 km, under the steep sides of the mountain ridges that plunge right into the sea, until we reach the village of Funningsfjørður at the end. This small village (population 70), strung out along the northern end of the fjord has a small quay and some fish farming.

Elduvík

To reach Elduvík, take R 634 past the scattered settlement of Funningsfjørður that lies at the head of the bay. R 634 follows the lower contours of the long mountain Hægstafjall (721 m) along the eastern shore of the fjord. This journey affords some spectacular views of the many parallel cirques on the opposite shore that have produced an unusual row of triangular ridges, facing the sea.

At the point of Elduvíksnes we have an excellent sight of the tiny village of Funningur at the base of a huge cirque, as well as the high mountain of Slættaratindur above it. This is a superb vantage point as you can see both up and down the fjord. At the northern tip at Múlin is the triangular-shaped mountain of Tyril (535 m) silhouetted against the sky. To the north-east, are the undulating mountains that constitute Kalsoy, while behind are the high peaks of Kunoy.

After a few more bends in the road, we are poised above the little village of Elduvík (population 50). The white-painted wooden church with its black roof dates from 1951 but is built in the traditional style. A river flows through the village which has some old turf-roofed houses besides some other houses from earlier this century, painted green, yellow, red and black.

No real harbour exists here since the village faces north and is quite unprotected. A landing place has been made in a cleft, with steps down to the sea. A large, wide valley cuts all the way back to Funningsfjørður, and along this is the old footpath that once connected the two villages.

You have to return the same way as you came, but the reward is spectacular scenery all the way until you are back on R 662. From here you can continue on to join R 10 and either return to the bridge via the tunnel or go on to Skálafjørður.

TRAIL 1: SUNDALAGSBRÚGVIN TO OYNDNARFJØRÐUR

Oyndnarfjørður

R 645 leads to Oyndnarfjørður and is approached by turning off R 10 to the north-west of Skálafjørður, depending on the way you came – directly from the bridge or via Eiði. R 645 climbs up through a narrow valley between Múlatindur (788 m) on the left and Blábjorg (731 m) on the right. The pass at 300 m can be shrouded in mist but, if not, there is a magnificent panoramic view forwards as the valley opens up. The village of Oyndnarfjørður is down to the left and Hellur to the right of the rectangular fjord, while in front are the ridged mountains of Kalsoy, with those of Kunoy behind.

Our road then snakes down the hillside before it forks: R 645 goes to the left to Oyndnarfjørður and R 647 to Hellur on the right. At the foot of the valley is a large wind generator that serves a huge inland fish farm. Taking R 645, and just where the road divides and before the cattle grid outside Oyndnarfjørður (population 160), a path leads down to the shore where the two famous rocking stones (*Rinkusteinar*) are to be found in the sea. These stones are moved by the waves – sometimes. Various rods and pieces of string are supposed to demonstrate these movements and you may be lucky and see them move!

The lower road leads down to the harbour while the upper

road goes through the higher part of the village. It has a large mole and a fish farm beyond it, while at the harbour quay is a fish factory. The old harbour, with its accompanying old houses and boat sheds, is on the other side of the new mole, while between them is the old church from 1838. It is of white painted wood with a turf roof and has a graveyard surrounded by a stone wall. Unlike similar churches from the same period this one has an exceptionally well-carved screen, with painted blue ends to the pews.

Most of the houses in the upper half of the village are quite new but above the new harbour is an old merchant's house (*Vikarhúsini*), with brown walls and a turf roof, which is now a museum. At the extreme end of the village is the Youth Hostel, *Fjallsgarður*, open all the year round.

We can see across to the long mountainous island of Kalsoy, opposite the fjord's mouth. On the other side of the fjord is the small village of Hellur that is reached by going round the end of the fjord and taking R 647.

Hellur has only about 20 oldish houses, no church and no harbour. It has a clear view across to Oyndnarfjørður and the mountain Tindur (504 m) above it.

TRAIL J: SUNDALAGSBRÚGVIN TO SELATRAÐ

This particular journey takes us all the way round the southern tongue of the Eysturoy peninsula from Skálafjørður to Selatrað and back again: a total distance of 45 km that passes through seven villages and hamlets. Before 1976, when the tunnel and bridge were both built, a ferry from Selatrað to Hósvík connected Eysturoy and Streymoy. R 10 from the bridge gets us quickly to Skálafjørður.

At the head of Skálafjørður is a small village of the same name, though it is sometimes known as Skálabotn. This fjord is the longest in the Faroes, being some 12 km in length. It served as a naval base for the British during the war.

We take off from R 10 and proceed south via R 69 from the petrol station at the village of Skálafjørður, consisting of a couple of dozen dispersed dwellings and a power station. There is a sandy ayre or spit at the point where the river Fjarðará, flowing from the valley in which Oyndnarfjørður lies, runs out into the fjord. A large water meadow has developed at this point. At one time there was an old *ting* place here.

Skáli

Proceeding south we first come to Skáli, after a long deserted stretch of road, and also to a choice between the lower road through the village or the upper by-pass road. The 650 people here are mainly employed by the shipbuilding and repair yard. It has a good harbour and a dry dock besides a fish factory. The church, near to the shipyard, was erected in 1940 from concrete; it is painted white with a corrugated red roof and has a clock, unusually, on the tower, maybe because it is in an industrial village. It might be added that sirens are used to call people to work, besides announcing the mid-day break in Tórshavn and other places.

Only a little way out of Skáli we come to the next hamlet called Innan Glyvur which is opposite Glyvrar, on the other side of the fjord. This dispersed settlement has mainly modern houses. There are many ring-nets for fish farming on this side of the fjord.

The next village is við Sjógv. It has a quay and a lopsided graveyard that is best seen from the other shore. The old black church with turf roof is L-shaped (an obvious later extension) since this is actually one of the oldest traditional churches in the Faroes – built in 1834. It is unpainted inside and has a carved screen that is well worth seeing. This is the parish church for the whole district.

Strendur

We now come to the more densely built-up village of Strendur (population 800) which is really a continuation of við Sjógv. It is connected to Toftir by frequent ferries to Tórshavn. A modern road at the lower level leads to a large harbour with a fish factory and also the ferry terminal, with many small boathouses beyond the harbour. Just above the terminal is a wool-spinning factory, *Snældan*, in a concrete building with a corrugated iron roof, next to a yellow-painted old house, where you can buy wool and also finished sweaters.

Beyond the village, to the south, is the point, Raktangi,

where a granite memorial (1976) within a white-walled enclosure has been erected to those lost at sea. It is possible to drive to the end of this point where Tangafjørður and Skálafjørður meet. Here we get a superb panorama all round: up Sundini, Kollafjørður and Skálafjørður, besides to the northern part of Nólsoy and Hvítanes, as well as seeing Tórshavn's waste-disposal unit, which looks more like a modern cathedral with a triangular base and a tall blue spire – one devoted to cleaner living?

Selatrað

R 669 swings around this point and goes in a north-west direction up the side of the fjord where we pass a few houses at Kolbanargjógv. Further along are several waterfalls flowing down the hillsides, before we come to Morskranes village which has a dozen or so houses and lies opposite the tip of Kollarfjørður. Eventually we reach Selatrað, after which the road goes no further, since this was once (but no longer) the ferry terminal to Hósvík on Streymoy.

Selatrað village (population 80) lies on relatively flat land near a small bay. The harbour lies by a small promontory which has on it an old black house that was once a shop. The church lies not far away and is of white concrete with a slate roof, built in 1927. This was once the *ting*-place for all Eysturoy.

A plantation of mixed trees at the end of the village was set up at the turn of the century, at the same time as the one in Tórshavn. It was not damaged so much as the Tórshavn plantation by the hurricanes of 1988–9. From here it is possible to see right down the sound to the tip of Nólsoy. Distances never seem very great in the Faroes and islands always appear to be quite close.

TRAIL K: SUNDALAGSBRÚGVIN TO NES

R 10 from the bridge actually runs along the eastern side of Skálafjørður from the top of the bay right down to Runavík, which is the name for both the village itself and the *kommune* that embraces most of the smaller villages down this coast of the fjord. Although these villages are individually signposted they are, in effect, almost contiguous along the shoreline. The total population is 2,400, which, if taken with the 1,150 in the neighbouring *kommune* of Nes, gives a total of 3,550 for the eastern shore. This dramatic increase in the local population is due simply to better communications with Tórshavn in recent years.

Sóldafjørður

Starting at the village of Skálafjørður, where R 10 begins to go round the top of the fjord and under the sloping green hillsides, there is a distance of 5 km before we reach to the first village: Gøtueiði. This small community has been absorbed by its southern neighbour, Skipanes, to give a combined population of 80 people. The road now divides and a sharp bend allows R 70 to climb back up the hill towards Leirvík. R 10, however, now enters a more populated village called Søldafjørður with about 300 people clustered along the road. Between the road and the water is a small plantation with four large, greyish oil tanks, protected in concrete and surrounded by a high barbed wire fence. During the war this fjord was used as a naval base. The sagas claim that Søldafjørður was founded by the brothers Skeggi and Sølmundur, the sons of Tróndur Tóralvsson and Oluva Tórsteinsdotter, the daughter of the Scottish-based Tórstein the Red. Skeggi, who was eldest, had the farm but he was thrown off a cliff by Sølmundur who then had to flee into exile. It was this Skeggi who was the ancestor of the Gøtuskeggi in Gøta, renowned in the Faroese saga.

Lambi

A welcome gap in the housing occurs along the road, under the steep sides of Stórafjall (567 m), until we come to a large quarry eating into the mountain. A road, R 683, then turns left towards Lambi on the other side of an isthmus. A number of new houses have been built at Lambareiði immediately along R 683, but further on, at Lambi, is a tight cluster of old houses, just before the bay. The total population is over 100. A mole and quay with several boathouses are situated at the head of this wide fjord of Lambavík. The arms of the fjord slope steeply into the water and have no habitation along them, although a lighthouse is placed at the tip of the northern arm. It was here, on New Year's Eve in 1708, that the Danish East India Company's boat *Norske Løve* was stranded in the bay, and the wreck is still buried here. Many proposals have been made to dig the boat out but it is hardly worthwhile, since most of the valuables were saved. The ship's bell now hangs in the old church at Tórshavn, together with a model of the boat, given by one of the grateful crew.

Glyvrar

Returning back to R 10 and proceeding south we come to the beginning of the most densely populated area along Skálafjørður, starting with Glyvrar, which has well over 400 people, tightly packed in houses along rows of roads. Down by the shore is an unusual church. It was originally built in 1927 of white stone with a brown corrugated iron roof when the population, of what is now Runavík, was only 800. The threefold expansion in population numbers required that the church also be expanded, and so it was, in 1981, by adding two more roofed buildings parallel and identical to the original.

Runavík

It is hard to tell when the next village, Saltangará, really begins, except that its 600 inhabitants have spread their houses even further up the hillside. Numerous shops of all types line the main road. Finally we reach Runavík at the head of a small bay with its 400 inhabitants. It has a large harbour and a number of fish factories and other industrial works. Thus, the *kommune* of Runavík is a long 6-km ribbon-development of mainly new houses and shops, with one hotel for good measure.

Rituvík

South of the village of Runavík is a road, R 685, that swings around the small Vatnfelli (166 m) towards Rituvík (population 200), which also belongs to the *kommune*. Passing a large lake, Toftavatn, to the right and shortly after, in the bend, we have a small road to the right to Æðuvík, over this low moorland. R 685 goes down to the small bay at Rituvík (the

Bay of the Kittiwake) on the east coast which has no beach and only a couple of steep slipways for the boats. The houses lie away from the shore since it is subject to heavy breakers. The small church has white wooden walls and a red roof and was built in 1953. Nearby, in a small enclosure, is a bronze statue of a couple looking out to sea, recalling those lost at sea. At the upper end of the village are two long buildings that comprised the large hen-batteries that used to provide the Faroes with eggs, though these are now defunct. Nólsoy can be seen to the south from here.

Returning back up to the road junction and taking R 687 we cross the moors above Toftavatn, from where it is possible to see over Skálafjørður. We come to another junction and take the left-hand road. Just before we come to Æðuvík we pass Tinghella, a flat rocky place where the first *ting* meetings on Eysturoy were held. The road winds down to Æðuvík (the Bay of the Eider-duck) where a small village, like at Rituvík, is well above and away from the coast. The population is about 70 but it has no harbour, only a steep slipway for the boats.

Climbing back up the road to the first junction we turn left along R 682 across the plateau (138 m), past some small lakes before a sharp, twisty descent takes us to Nes and Toftir, on the shore below. Not surprisingly, excellent vistas exist here, up the various fjords as well as to the outskirts of Tórshavn to the south.

It is possible to come down off the hills to Nes, as described above, or to approach it from Runavík along R 10. In the latter case, the road goes round the bay out of Runavík village, around the next promontory, before coming to the small village of Saltnes, which has over 100 people.

Toftir

After a short break, we come to the large ferry terminal at Toftir with nearly 800 people, whose houses are built up in layers below the 129-m high hill Húslongd. The frequent car ferry *Dúgvan* (The Dove) links up Toftir with Strendur on the other side, *en route* to Tórshavn, which is a far quicker journey than the option of travelling all the way round by road. The harbour is large and has a fish processing plant. In the opposite direction the road climbs out of Toftir towards Nes and at the top, on the left-hand side, is a memorial to those lost at sea. It represents a woman and child looking out over the fjord but, intriguingly, it is made out of spaced strips of metal, which means you can see right through them, from all directions!

Nes

If we continue south along R 689 we come down to Nes (population 225) whose parish and *kommune* once included all the villages up the eastern side of Skálafjørður but is now restricted to just Nes, Toftir and Saltnes. The church is an old one, built in 1843, and is of classical traditional style with black wooden walls but with a slate roof. The screen is exceptionally well carved and it is all unpainted inside. It and its graveyard are surrounded by a stone wall and are well worth seeing. Below the church is a small landing place with a steep slipway. Nearby is the old manse which may be made into a museum. The road eventually peters out at a farm. From this point, it seems hardly any distance to Tórshavn – 5 km across the sound.

TRAIL L: SUNDALAGSBRÚGVIN TO FUGLAFJØRÐUR

At Gøtueiði on R 10 from the bridge towards Toftir, the other road, R 70 cuts back sharply northwards up the hillside until it reaches the top of the pass. Here, a stop should be made, for on this flat, breathtaking place many religious, revivalist mass meetings were held in the past during the summer, when the people lived there in tents. The reason for choosing this site for uplifting meetings is plain to see before you, as you look over the fjords and mountains to the north-west. Below, lie the three villages of Gøta *kommune* (975 people): Syðrugøta, Gøtugjógv and Norðragøta with their large infields, now largely built over.

Descending down past Syðrugøta (population 400) along the new road, it is necessary to double back at the end of the village in order to enter it. A sprinkling of older houses cluster around the small bay while the newer houses are up in the once-precious infield. No harbour, to speak of, exists as it has such an exposed position. The largest spinning mill in the Faroes, *Tøtingavirkið*, is located here and can be visited on request. It is said that the saga hero Tróndur úr Gøta built a church here, but this seems most unlikely since he fought against the Christian warrior, Sigmundur Brestirson, and eventually killed him.

Norðragøta

R 70 continues to Gøtugjógv (population 60) near a fissure, or gjógv, where the central school is located and a new church has been built for the whole *kommune*. After this, the road swings round Eggin (347 m) and heads up the valley to the north-west. However, a road to the right goes to Norðragøta (population 500) which is well worth a visit since this is the place where that Viking chief Tróndur lived and where, it is said, you can see the remains of his house.

The church was built in 1833 and is, hence, one of the twelve oldest surviving churches in the Faroes. It has all the traditional features: tarred wooden walls, turf roof and white tower, a well-carved screen and unpainted wooden pews. But what will become of it, with a new, larger church at Gøtugjógv?

Blásastova is Norðragøta's folk museum. It was once a farmhouse and was built at the same time as the church. It is surrounded by some charming buildings, with turf roofs, that were erected at the turn of the century. This is one of the best-equipped folk museums in the Faroes and displays everything that could be expected on such a farm from the nineteenth century.

At Norðragøta, the sheltered harbour serves the whole community and has a large fish processing factory. Agriculture, today, is not as important as industry and so, again, we find the infield given over to new modern buildings.

Just beyond the village, the road swings sharply right and up to the tunnel through the mountain. The tunnel was opened in 1985 and has a lighted dual carriageway for 2.3 km that carries you through to Leirvík, on the other side of the northern arm of the bay of Gøtuvík.

Leirvík

Leirvík village (population 830) is situated on the lower slopes of Sigatindur (613 m) on the northern side of Gøtuvík. The colourful array of houses are closely built in rising, semicircular rows above the large harbour with its fish factory. Nearby is the church (1906) of white-painted stone with a black roof. It was recently extended to cope with the increased population but has preserved its original design with arched windows. In the nearby old graveyard are preserved the remains of a medieval Catholic church. Below the church are rows of black boathouses along the shore, opposite the ferry terminal to Klaksvík. To the east end of the village is a memorial to those who perished at sea; it is brutally made in the form of a sinking boat. Further east still is the local communal incinerator with a tall blue chimney.

Leirvík is directly opposite the end of Kalsoy, with its high mountain of Gríslatindur (703 m) and the higher ridges beyond. We can see right to the western end of Borðoy from here.

An old road (before the tunnel was built) is at the top, western end of the village and crosses over the beginning of the tunnel and around the northern contours of Leirvíksfjørður. Up the slopes of the infield are many examples of the old terracing techniques of cultivation.

We take the old (unnumbered) and discredited road out of Leirvík. It is not now reckoned to be part of the road network because of the number of rockfalls there that have cut the road off many times. The reason for coming this way is simply to visit the only hot spring in the Faroes, but it is always possible to avoid this road and use the tunnel. From the old road grand views up Fuglafjørður are to be had, as well as across to Kalsoy and the green fields of Blankskáli. The latter village was devastated by an avalanche and the people moved to Syðradalur, on the other side of the island.

Before reaching R 65 to Fuglafjørður, we come to a forlorn cairn by the side of the road, on the right hand, with the inscription '*Varmakelda*' (Hot spring). From there, it is anyone's guess where to go down the slippery fields, but keep a look out for the odd cairn and the occasional stick, which are supposed to guide you there. Actually you go in a north-westerly direction towards Fuglafjørður, if you can. Eventually, down by the shore is the final cairn, where a small circular pool is to be found, bubbling away at about 18° C. This is not a hot, but only a warm spring.

Returning to the road, until it meets R 65 to Fuglafjørður, where, turning right, we get an excellent view of the beautiful south-western-facing fjord. After a little way, we come to a new village in the making, on the left – Kambsdalur – which has a number of industrial buildings besides a cafeteria, a sports hall and many modern houses.

Fuglafjørður

It is then only a couple of kilometres, past several waterfalls, until the outskirts of Fuglafjørður village, with its 1,700 inhabitants, are reached. A long quay on the north side has both fish factories and a fish meal plant. A marina is just below the middle of the village, while above that is an astonishingly modern church with a separate bell tower, erected in 1984. The church has a steep sloping turf roof as has the belfry – a novel but satisfying design in these surroundings. The old church was pulled down, but some of the older houses are still in the vicinity, with flourishing gardens. Older boathouses are just above the marina, where the village had its origins. There is a small plantation behind an old black-painted house. Because the village lies in a cirque between Slættafjall (626 m) and Húsafelli (627 m), as at Leirvík the houses are staggered up the cirque valley in half a dozen semicircular rows.

Returning down the road and proceeding along R 65, a splendid vista is then obtained over the valley in which the village of Norðragøta lies, before we rejoin R 70.

NORÐOYAR

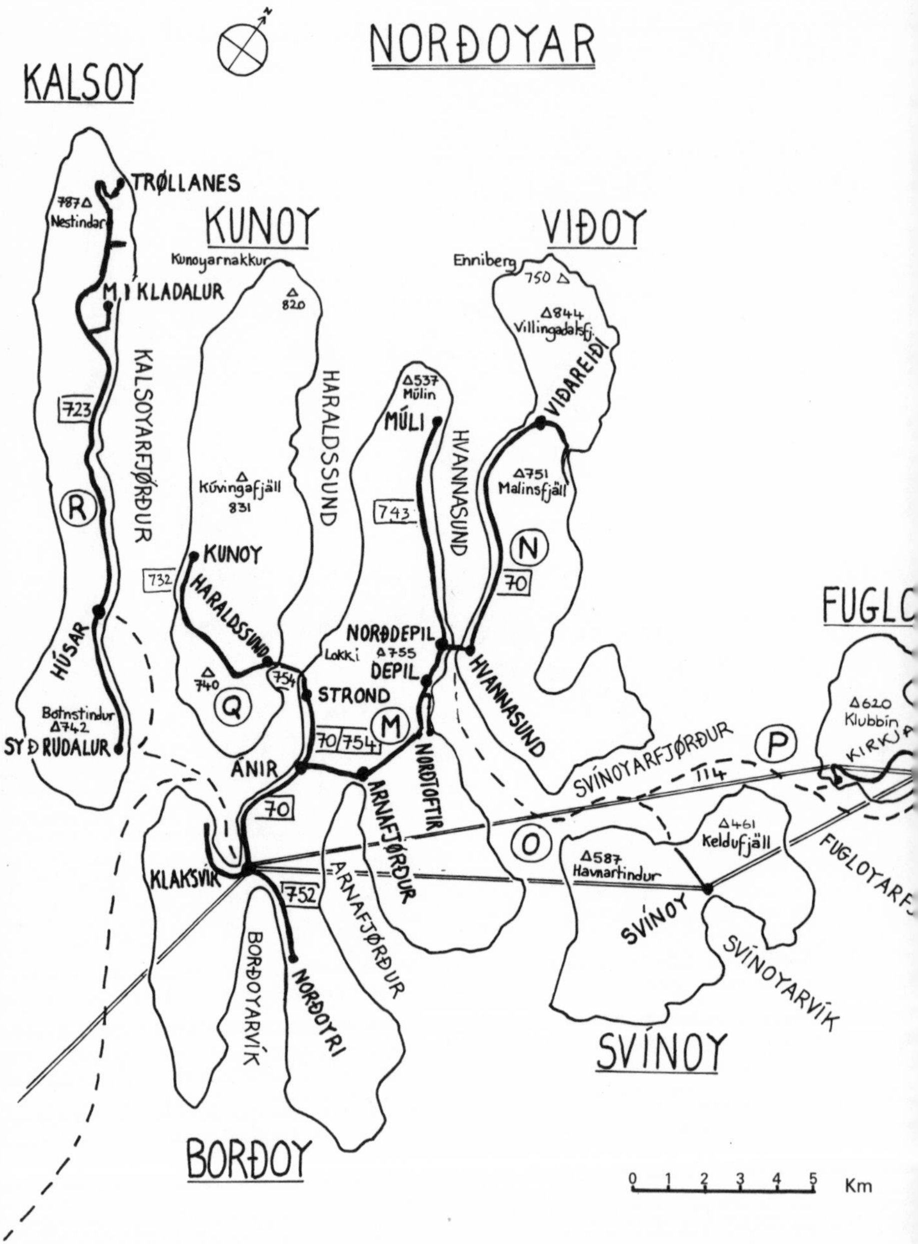

KALSOY

KUNOY

VIÐOY

FUGL

787△ Nestindar
TRØLLANES
M.I KLADALUR
Kunoyarnakkur
820△
Enniberg
750 △
△844 Villingadalsfj.
△537 Múlin
723
R
KALSOYARFJØRÐUR
HARALDSSUND
MÚLI
HVANNASUND
VIÐAREIÐI
△751 Malinsfjall
△620 Klubbin
Kúvingafjäll 831
743
N
70
KIRKJ
732
KUNOY
HARALDSSUND
NORÐDEPIL
△755 DEPIL
Lokki
HÚSAR
740△
754
HVANNASUND
Q
STROND
SVÍNOYARFJØRÐUR
T14
P
Botnstindur △742
SYÐRUDALUR
ÁNIR
70/754
M
NORÐTOFTIR
ARNAFJØRÐUR
O
△461 Keldufjäll
FUGLOYARFJ
70
△587 Havnartindur
KLAKSVÍK
752
ARNAFJØRÐUR
SVÍNOY
SVÍNOYARVÍK
BORÐOYARVÍK
NORÐOYRI
SVÍNOY
BORÐOY
0 1 2 3 4 5 Km

Island Work

Sunday fishing: This popular sport is taking place in Tórshavn, somewhat unfairly outside the fish-factory where offal is discharged and attracts many fish.

Sandur: Here we have an example of a modern fish-processing factory and its harbour.

Fuglafjørður: Although this captures the heyday of modern fish-meal production, it shows the importance of the fish industry to the survival of the Faroes. See Chapter 15.

Tórshavn ship-builders: Ship-building and repair can be profitable, but that is never certain in the Faroes when all the raw material has to be imported.

Syðradal: Here we have the small village perched high above the cliffs and breakers, with the boat-houses and landing-place down by the shore. See Chapter 16.

Fuglafjørður: This photo is a reminder of the past, before the modern factories came.

16 Norðoyar: the Northern Isles

The six small islands in the north are collectively known as Norðoyar. They are characterized by the many strong currents between the islands and their high peaks that give them a rugged and untamed appearance, not found elsewhere in the Faroes. These conditions mean that this total area of 240.77 sq. km has relatively few inhabitants outside the large town of Klaksvík on Borðoy. Their isolation has produced a strong local dialect and sense of identity, but their remoteness is now ameliorated by the introduction of better modes of transport: roads, tunnels, causeways, ferries and helicopters. Improved communications have also halted the slump in population.

Borðoy

This is the biggest island in the northern group and has an area of 94.90 sq. km. It is separated from Viðoy by Hvannasund, although it now has a causeway. Over Haraldssund another causeway joins Borðoy to Kunoy, while Kalsoyarfjørður divides the island off from Kalsoy. Borðoy is 21 km from north to south and is 10 km at its broadest. The northernmost peak is Múlin (537 m), and below it is the tiny hamlet of Múli with only three houses, but now a road connects them to Klaksvík, the largest town/village in the north with 4,850 people. Towards the south, the island is split into three peninsulas by two fjords, Árnafjørður and Borðoyarvík, which appear to be three separate islands when viewed from the sea. At the end of Árnafjørður is a village of the same name, with some 90 inhabitants. The head of Borðoyarvík is joined by an isthmus (18 m over sea level) to the bay, Vágur, where Klaksvík lies. Otherwise, high coasts are found all around the highest point being Lokki (755 m) in the middle of the island.

Two tunnels connect Klaksvík to the other side of the island where the villages of Norðtoftir, Depil and Norðdepil lie, near Hvannasund, that have a total population of 250.

TRAIL M: KLAKSVÍK TO MÚLI

Two sea routes exist to Klaksvík: direct from Tórshavn by the car ferry *Teistin* or her sister ship *Smyril*, which takes an hour or so, or via R 10 to Lervík and then by *Ternan* on her half-hour journey. In both cases you sail round the triangular cliffs at the ends of Kalsoy and Kunoy which lie away from you in a north-north-easterly direction, like both Borðoy and Viðoy themselves. This journey takes you down a fjord, well protected by mountain ranges on both sides, to the second largest settlement in the Faroes, on the island of Borðoy. It is also possible to fly direct from Tórshavn by helicopter.

Klaksvík

Klaksvík has nearly 5,000 inhabitants and their dwellings stretch up both sides of the fjord in parallel layers. On the left side, as we sail past, are the quays and fish factories belonging to Kjølbro's, the largest private fishing company in the Faroes. The rise of the fishing industry here began at the turn of the century but gained prominence only with the decline of fishing in Suðeroy in the 20s. Today it has the largest fishing harbour in the Faroes.

The old centre of the small town of Klaksvík is sited on a low piece of land or isthmus between the bay where the boats dock and the long fjord of Borðoyarvík, on the other side. A number of old black-painted houses lie near the ends of both fjords, as well as many small boat sheds by the shore. Between these sheds on the western shore of Borðoyarvík excavations (still continuing) have revealed a number of ancient Viking house sites.

In Klaksvík they have a large modern church (1963) that is unusual in not having a tower but having a separate bell tower. It was designed by a Danish architect to reflect a mixture of modern and traditional architecture and may be said to resemble the unfinished Magnus cathedral in Kirkjubøur. It is made of local stone with a slate roof and large vertical windows. Christians-Kirkjan, as it is known, has a large fresco altar piece from Viborg cathedral in Denmark as well as a 4,000-year-old pagan sacrificial altar from Denmark that is now used as a font. Another unusual feature is the old 'áttamanfar', or eight-man boat, hanging from the ceiling that was used to carry the minister from Viðareiði. A new fountain has been put up near the church and was designed by the Faroese artist Fridtjov Joensen.

A museum has been made out of the old Monopoly ware-house on the west side of the town along Klaksvíksvegur, near to the harbour where the Tórshavn boat docks. When this warehouse was established in 1838, the village was called Vágur. To avoid confusion with the other Vágur in Suðeroy, the name of the village was changed to Klaksvík in 1911. This Vágur was originally the site of the old *ting* for the Northern Isles.

From the southern part of the bay we have a good overview of the village and its harbour. In the distance stands the triangular outline of the island of Kunoy which protects the bay from northern winds.

Continuing south along R 752, down Borðoyarvík to Norðoyri, with its 40 inhabitants, lying under Høgahædd (563 m), the road passes the hamlet of Gerðar with the overgrown ruins of a large farm that was destroyed by an avalanche in 1745. The buildings were quickly restored but twenty years later it was again overwhelmed by another avalanche. A memorial stone was put up to mark these unfortunate events.

Taking R 70 northwards, but branching off left on the R 754, the road passes the tiny hamlet of Ánir and comes to the hydro-electricity works at Strond. This road leads on to Kunoy over a causeway at the narrowest point of the sound.

Following R 70 north out of Klaksvík to Múli you by-pass Ánir to enter one of the two tunnels across Borðoy. A large white arrow shows precedence, while the red arrow tells you to give way at the meeting places, marked with a large white M, and to draw into the side alcoves. Emerging from the first tunnel built in 1967 a small road, R 756, to the right goes winding down to the small village of Árnafjørður (population 90) along the north side of the fjord. It has a little sandy beach, a large quay and a fish factory, plus a fish farm in the bay. The small church was erected in 1937 with white walls and a black roof, and lies at the beginning of the village.

Returning up the hill, the road enters the second tunnel, and emerges high up, with a good prospect over to Viðoy as well as to the small villages of Norðdepil and Hvannasund below. The R 70 descends steeply to the shores of Hvannasund but just before the bottom of the road we find a sharp turn off to the right. This road, R 758, leads to Norðtoftir, which has only a couple of houses but a large fish farm onshore and ring-nets in the fjord. From here, the village of Hvannasund on Viðoy can be glimpsed across the water, as well as the rocky face of Svínoy down the sound.

Rejoining R 70, we enter Depil with its half a dozen houses, amongst which is a well-preserved traditional black-sided, turf-roofed farmhouse by the side of the road. The hamlet is at the bottom of a cirque called Húsadalur. A little further on is a road to Norðdepil, to the right along the shore, but R 70 by-passes it.

Norðdepil has a population of over 250 and this large number can be attributed to the damming of the sound that led to better connections between Viðoy and Borðoy. Before this recent event there was a small ferry here to Hvannasund which, today, only maintains the ferry connections to Svínoy and Fugloy. It is thus a nexus for the three northernmost islands. The village has both a harbour and a hotel. Driving straight out of Norðdepil, the road goes to the school but no further.

It is 13 km to Múli and back again along R 743, along the side of north Borðoy, which is a series of cirques coming down from a 700-m ridge that forms the central spine of the island. This is quite dissimilar to the relatively smoothly sloping sides of Viðoy, to the right. Both the road to Múli and that to Viðareiði, on the other side, run almost parallel up the sides of the sound, well above the water. The three houses that constitute Múli are set high up, on a green shelf above the rocks below, for it has no immediate landing place. However, further south is a path leading down to a boathouse by the shore, where the inhabitants could row across the sound to another small landing place at Leiti on Viðoy. Both these places were used before the road was driven through to Múli in 1989, although they did have a helicopter connection for a short while.

From Múli we get a superb picture of Viðareiði, nestling under the huge cirque formed from Villingadalsfjall (844 m). Múli lies at the tip of Borðoy, under its own cirque formed from Múlin (537 m). The reason for making this expensive, long road to just a handful of people was said to preserve the hamlet from becoming extinct. Whether this political decision pays off in the long run remains to be seen, but it seems to be working.

Viðoy

This island has an area of 41.1 sq. km. It is separated from Borðoy on the west by Hvannasund but a causeway now joins the two islands. To the south-east, Svínoyarfjørður separates it from Svínoy. A deep southern inlet called Viðvík is found on the east coast. At the northern end are the perpendicular cliffs of Enniberg (755 m), the northernmost point in the Faroes. At the foot of these cliffs are many stacks that stand over 100 m high. The highest peak is Villingadalsfjall (844 m), also in the north of the island.

Viðoy is generally high apart from the isthmus, in the north, on which the village of Viðareiði (population 300) lies, beneath a vast cirque. This is well known for being exposed to heavy breakers and therefore it has landing places on both sides of the island, as well as a small pier at Leiti, some 3 km south of the village along the sound, Hvannasund, which is a safe place in all weathers. South of the village is the high Malinsfjall (751 m).

Hvannasund is also the name of the only other village, further south on Viðoy where a causeway goes across to Norðdepil, on the other side on Borðoy.

TRAIL N: KLAKSVÍK TO VIÐAREIÐI

R 70 crosses the causeway at Norðdepil, with the village of Hvannasund lying immediately to the right under a sloping mountainside. Its population of 250 lives along the western shore of Viðoy, in gaily coloured houses by the quay. The church is at the end of the village near the shore and is a small white concrete construction, with a red corrugated iron roof, dating from 1949. This village and Norðdepil, on the other side, form a single *kommune*. Both are very exposed and subject to strong winds that blow up the sound. It is from here that the ferry to Svínoy and Fugloy departs nowadays.

Viðareiði

Going across the causeway at Hvannasund, R 70 turns left and along the side of the sloping sides of Viðoy to the northernmost village in the Faroes – Viðareiði. The scenery across the sound to Borðoy is spectacular. After some 8 km we round the bend into Viðareiði (population 300), one of the most beautifully situated villages in the Faroes. As the name suggests, the village is on an isthmus (*eiði*) and lies between Villingardalsfjall (844 m) to the north and Malinsfjall (751 m) to the south.

The church lies to the left, near the coast. It is a white stone walled church with a slate roof dating from 1892. The church is well endowed with altar silver – a gift from the British Government for the help shown towards the crew of the brig *Marwood* which was wrecked off the coast in 1847. The most noteworthy object in the church is a late Gothic crucifix given to the church in 1551 by the Hamburg merchant Thomas Koppen, who once held the trade monopoly. Nearby is the old turf-roofed manse built in the traditional style. Only a poor landing place exists on the western side.

A hotel is to be found at the top of the village. On the eastern side of the isthmus there is a landing place and a steep slipway for boats. From here we have an excellent sight of Fugloy over the waters. A small road goes a couple of kilometres south along the coast to Dalar where, at the bottom of a narrow cirque, is a fish farm. The mountain stream, Dalá, feeds these fish tanks.

Svínoy

'Swine Island' has no pigs on it today but it may well have done in the past. It lies south of Fugloy and has an area of 27.35 sq. km. It is 8 km from north-west to south-east and 6 km from east to west. An isthmus, just 34 m above sea level, divides the island in two: the harbour on the west side serves the village on the east side with its population of 60. To the north is the peak of Keldufjall (461 m) and to the south Havnartindur (587 m).

160 THE FAROES *The Faraway Islands*

TRAIL O: HVANNASUND TO SVÍNOY

Másin (the Herring Gull) leaves Hvannasund for the journey to Svínoy along the sound. The cliffs get steeper as the boat proceeds along, with Sneis (634 m) on Viðoy to the left, Tólvmarkaknúkur (620 m) on Borðoy to the right, while ahead are the cliffs of Havnartindur (587 m) on Svínoy. The ferry always tows a small flit-boat behind it because sometimes it is difficult to tie up at the quays.

The little ferry rounds the point of Viðoy and progresses up Svínoyfjørður along the rugged coastline of Svínoy with its bird-cliffs. The boat docks at Svínoyareiði on the isthmus where a 1-km long road leads to the village of Svínoy (population 60). The church (1878) is made of white stone walls and a corrugated iron roof. In the churchyard is an old gravestone with a simple cross called *Bjarnasteinur* which was discovered under the previous church in 1828. This stone is traditionally held to be that of Svínoy-Bjarni who was the mother's brother of Tróndur úr Gøta. The village has a fairly large infield, besides a helipad.

Fugloy

'Bird Island' is the smallest island in the northern group with an area of 11.18 sq. km. It is separated from its neighbour Svínoy by the strong currents of Fugloyfjørður. It is 5 km from north to south and from east to west. The highest peak is Klubbin (620 m) while to the east is the tall stack, Stapi, with the easternmost lighthouse in the Faroes. The two villages of Kirkja and Hattarvík are connected by road and have a total population of 60. As the name suggests, there is a rich bird life here and the inhabitants pursue their traditional custom of fowling more than on other islands.

TRAIL P: HVANNASUND TO FUGLOY

Proceeding to Fugloy on *Másin*, the boat leaves Svínoyareiði and heads north past the bird-cliffs of Keldufjall (461 m) on the right. A band of dark, possibly bituminous deposits can be seen half way up the rockface but it is too inaccessible to be worked. Crossing Fugloyarfjørður, we get a fine view of Viðareiði opposite, under the massive mountaintop of Villingadalsfjall (844 m). Beyond it, and just out of sight, is the massive promontory of Enniberg (750 m) at the tip of Viðoy that falls vertically into the sea.

Kirkja

We are soon in sight of the village of Kirkja on the southern slopes of Fugloy that rise to the high peak of Klubbin (620 m). A sharply-raked set of steps leads down to an older landing stage to the west below the church but a newer, smaller quay has been built to the east and is approachable by road. It has a helipad for the regular flights that link Klaksvík, Svínoy and Fugloy to Tórshavn.

The church that gives its name to the village stands at the west end and just outside it. The church dates from 1933 but is in the traditional style with black stone walls and a green corrugated iron roof that was once turf-covered. The red, white and yellow houses mainly have green roofs as well, curiously enough.

From Kirkja a winding road, R 792, snakes its way over the steep mountainside to the other village of Hattarvík.

Hattarvík

Másin plies its way from the quay at Kirkja and hugs the steep coastline which is pierced by numerous caves caused by sea erosion. Hattarvík village is in a south-east facing bay and has an old landing stage as well as a new little quay. Considering that both villages have only a couple of dozen people each it is surprising that Hattarvík also has a church. It was erected in 1899 and has white stone walls with a green roof, and lies to the west, above the landing place. However, in 1930, when the new church was built in Kirkja, the total population was as great as 230, but today that population is only 60, shared equally between the two villages.

This small community has a large infield for growing hay and they have always had fowling along the bird-cliffs. Further along the coast is the most eastern point of the Faroes – Stapi – complete with lighthouse.

Kunoy

With an area of 35.46 sq. km, Kunoy is separated from Borðoy by Haraldssund, but now has a causeway, and from Kalsoy by Kalsoyarfjørður. It is 14 km from south-south-east to north-north-west but only 4 km wide and is, basically, a long chain of mountains that are 800 m high. At the northern end, the mountain Kunoyarnakkur falls almost vertically 820 m into the sea. The highest peak is Kúvingarfjall (831 m) in the middle of the island. By the causeway is the village of Haraldssund with some 40 people and, beyond that, through the longest tunnel in the Faroes is the village of Kunoy itself, on the west coast with 60 people, below a cirque.

TRAIL Q: KLAKSVÍK TO KUNOY

Along R 70, a turning off goes to Kunoy along R 754 that passes through Ánir and Strond on the west side of Borðoy, before crossing the causeway to Haraldssund. These two hamlets lie at the foot of the green, sloping and ridged cliffs of Borðoy itself.

At the left end of the causeway are some new houses but the actual village of Haraldssund itself is further to the right under the mountain ridge of Galvsskorafjall (740 m). The village is divided in two halves, with just a handful of houses in each half and some boathouses in between. The population is about 50 but may be expected to grow with this new link to Borðoy.

Further north of Haraldssund, along the fjord, is the deserted village of Skarð, some 5 km distant. It was abandoned when the Skarð boat with all its able-bodied men sank in 1913 and they drowned.

Kunoy

The village of Kunoy is reached by continuing south on R 754 above Haraldssund and through the 3-km tunnel that goes straight under the mountain Galvsskorafjall (740 m). The tunnel was opened in 1988 and is single track and unlit, with the usual meeting places. It is currently the longest in the Faroes and likely to remain so, since the only village not yet connected to the road network is Gásadalur on Vágar, and this will not require a long tunnel. Our road emerges on the western side of Kunoy immediately opposite Húsar village on Kalsoy. The now-renumbered road, R 732, proceeds a couple of kilometres along the side of Kalsoyarfjørður before coming to the village of Kunoy.

Kunoy village nestles tightly under a dramatic cirque coming down from the ridges that form a mountainous, 800-m high backbone to the island. There are quite a few trees, as well as a fir plantation, up where the stream, Myllá, comes down the mountain, through the village and past the church. The white-painted wooden church (1867), with its red corrugated iron roof, stands high above a small harbour below. The village has two separate clusters of houses: one by the church and the other a couple of hundred metres south of it. A curious feature of this village is that quite a lot of the houses have their date of construction painted on their walls. The little old school is thus dated 1886.

To the north a path goes through the infield, past a couple of old houses and a small hydro-electric power station. From this point we get a fascinating view over the length and breadth of Kalsoy and the road that connects up all these villages. Only Trøllanes village, at the very tip of Kalsoy, is not visible as it is hidden behind a promontory.

Kalsoy

The most western of these northern islands is Kalsoy, with an area of 30.87 sq. km. It is separated from Kunoy to the east by Kalsoyarfjørður and from Eysturoy by Djúpini and Leirvíksfjørður. It is 18 km long from south-east to north-west and barely 3 km across. The island is high and almost inaccessible on the west side for the steep cliffs forbid access except in the south. The eastern side, however, slopes down to the coast and a number of deep valleys provide shelter for the four villages on the island. From Syðradalur in the south to Trøllanes in the north, a road connects up all the villages, through several tunnels. The total population is 130. The highest peak is Nestindur (787 m), lying between the two northern villages of Mikladalur and Trøllanes, through which a tunnel connects these two villages. The highest peak in the south is Botnstindur (742 m).

TRAIL R: SYÐARADLUR TO TRØLLANES

Taking the very small ferry boat *Barskor* from Klaksvík to Kalsoy, you sail out of the bay and past the triangular end of Kunoy and hug the coast, before crossing over Kalsoyarfjørður to Húsar, because of the strong currents.

Húsar

Húsar village (population 40) is built up the rise from the shore. The church is on the left near the water and is constructed up the slope with a large cellar at the lower east end. The church (1920) is made of white-painted stone with a red roof. The old cultivation terraces and field system form a green backdrop to this small village. A fissure divides the village in two, with the church in one half and the quayside in the other. Numerous black *hjallur* or drying-sheds are located just along this dividing line. Black boat sheds (*neyst*) line the broad steps up from the small quay.

From Húsar R 723 connects together all the villages on Kalsoy, north and south.

Looking back across the sound towards Kunoy village, the entrance of the road runnel on Kunoy is clearly visible in the mountainside.

Syðradalur

Barskor also calls on Syðradalur on its way back to Klaksvík. A couple of houses and boat sheds are down by the shore but the rest of the village is perched 100 m or so higher up, looking down over the green infield. It has a difficult landing stage to get alongside.

Altogether a dozen houses with a population of just a dozen or so constitute the village. It was here that the people from Blankskáli on the other side of the mountain Botnstindur (743 m), which lowers over Syðradalur village, came to settle in 1809, after their village was destroyed by an avalanche.

It is possible to get here by road from Húsar, a couple of kilometres to the north, along R 723.

We can see up Kalsoyarfjørður towards Kunoy, as well towards the peaks of Borðoy.

Mikladalur

Mikladalur is now reached from Húsar by road, after passing through three short tunnels, some 9 km distant. Shortly after the third tunnel a take-off road goes to Mikladalur and swings into the village, which is well above the breakers.

The church (1915) has white stone walls and a red corrugated iron roof. The village has a dozen houses and some 50 inhabitants. It seems that the new road has stabilized a population that had begun to decline because of its isolation. However, it always had a large infield for feeding the sheep, on which the people relied.

Trøllanes

R 723 continues above Mikladalur and gives an interesting view down on the village, besides over the fjord to Kunoy, before it disappears into a straight 2.3-km tunnel, completed in 1985. A side tunnel to the right leads directly to Djúpadalur, a cirque lying beneath Nestindar (787 m) with good agricultural land. The main tunnel continues through the mountain until it emerges above Trøllanes.

Again we find only a dozen houses here and a score of people. The village is some way from the sea but a north-easterly wind can cause spray to fly right over the village. Again, the new road connections seem to be holding the people there.

From Trøllanes, or from the lighthouse at Kallur to the north, is a most imposing sight of the highest and steepest cliffs in all the Faroes: Kunoyarnakkur (820 m) and Enniberg (750 m) at the northern ends of Kunoy and Viðoy respectively. These headlands are the highest in Europe, possibly in the world – so they are well worth seeing.

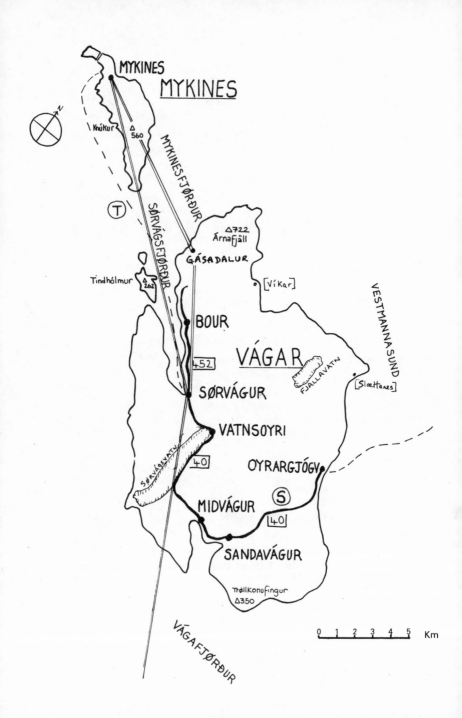

MYKINES

MYKINES

Knúkur △560

Ⓣ

△722
Árnafjáll

GÁSADALUR

Tindhólmur △262

○ [Víkar]

BOUR

VÁGAR

FJALLAVATN

[Slættanes]

SØRVÁGUR

VATNSOYRI

[40] OYRARGJÓGV

Ⓢ

MIDVÁGUR

[40]

SANDAVÁGUR

Trøllkonufingur
△350

MYKINESFJØRÐUR

SØRVÁGSFJØRÐUR

VESTMANNASUND

SØRVÁGSVATN

VÁGAFJØRÐUR

[52]

0 1 2 3 4 5   Km

17   Vágar and Mykines

Vágar

'The Bays' is a well suited name for this, the third largest island, since all the main villages are on bays and are named accordingly. It is 177.61 sq. km in area and has 2,900 inhabitants. It is separated from Streymoy by the 2-km stretch of Vestmannasund, over which constant ferries pass to and fro. Mykinesfjørður separates it from the island of Mykines. Vágar has an irregular coastline that is roughly 15 km from north to south and 22 km from east to west. On the south coast is a deep inlet that divides into two bays at Midvágur and Sandavágur, while to the west is a deep fjord that leads down to Sørvágur. A depression in the middle of the island extends from the deserted village of Víkar in the north to Bøsdalafossur (an impressive waterfall) in the south, giving rise to two lakes: Fjallavatn and the 6-km long Sørvágsvatn, also known as Leitisvatn. Nearby is the only airstrip in the Faroes. In the north-west the mountains are quite high, like the highest peak Árnafjall (722 m), that produce steep bird-cliffs in this part of the island, with accompanying stacks in the sea.

The stacks around Vágar are amongst the most spectacular in the whole of the Faroes. On the south-east coast beyond Sandavágur is the 313-m Trøllkonufingur (the Witch's Finger) also still known as Kongspiret (the King's Spire) after the visit of Crown Prince Fredrik in 1844. Outside Sørvágsfjørður is an array of stacks and holms worthy of mention: the two stacks of Drangarnir, one with a hole through it, Tindhólmur (262 m) with some fantastic peaks, and Gáshólmur (65 m).

In all the Faroes, only the village of Gásadalur is not connected by road, though there are plans for a tunnel! The relatively new village at the head of Sørvágsvatn, Vatnsoyrar, is the only inland village in the Faroes.

TRAIL S: OYRARGJÓGV TO BØUR

The ferry from Vestmanna lands you at Oyrargjógv on Vágar, which is not a village but simply a quayside. Plans have been put forward to build an underwater tunnel between Streymoy and Vágar to simplify transportation between the airport and the capital; however, this is still in the realms of speculation since an airport could always be built nearer Tórshavn, but it is all a question of finance. Meanwhile, the regular ferries *Sam* and *Ternan* (the Tern) ply the sound constantly every half hour.

Sandavágur

Eight km from the ferry quay we come to the fishing village of Sandavágur (population 760), to the left of R 40. It has only a small, exposed harbour with the church at the end of the bay, around which the gaily painted houses are situated. The former church was nearer the shore but was moved inland because of the danger from heavy breakers. The church, in the middle of the village, is large and modern, built in 1917, and can seat 250 worshippers. During the war it was attended by

British forces but those who died there on active service are buried outside Miðvágur. Unlike most churches in the Faroes it is cheerfully decorated inside. It also contains a rare rune stone that was found just when the church was consecrated. This large stone, dating from the thirteenth century, declares at the bottom: '*Torkil Onandarson, from Rogaland* (south-west Norway) *founded this place*'.

Near the harbour is a large rectangular monument to V. U. Hammershaimb (the inventor of the Faroese script) who was born here, at á Steig, in 1819.

Miðvágur

Past Sandavágur lies Miðvágur, which stretches for a couple of kilometres in an east-west direction, above a sheltered bay which is the basis for the fishing prosperity of its 1,100 inhabitants. It has a large, safe harbour and a marina. The bay is renowned for its high percentage of pilot whale hunts because of its large, grey sandy beach, at ebb tide, onto which the whales are driven and quickly dispatched.

A hundred metres above this large, extended village is the famous minister's widow's house at Kalvalið. The fame belongs to the celebrated twentieth-century Faroese novelist Jörgen-Frantz Jacobsen's story *Barbara*. The story tells of a woman in the eighteenth century who married two clergymen, both of whom died mysteriously. The actual house lies low, almost buried, in the hillside, with a turf roof and stone walls. It is now a museum and contains a typical collection of quasi-medieval objects. The keys are kept down at the *kommune* office in the middle of the village.

The church, built in 1952 by a local architect, lies in the western part and is quite large. It is a white-painted concrete structure with a *Norwegian* slate roof and a high tower capped with a copper pinnacle; there is no similar church in the Faroes. The former wooden church, built in 1836, was pulled down in 1953. In the old churchyard is a memorial cross (1963) raised to those lost at sea. Further west is a small graveyard for fourteen British servicemen who died here during the war.

From Midvágur R 40 passes along the largest lake in the Faroes – Sørvágsvatn. This piece of water, also called

Leitisvatn, is 5.6 km long and almost 1 km broad. It is full of trout and the old boathouses nearby bear witness to profitable fishing here. At the southern end of the lake is a narrow neck of land that keeps back the water and over which there is a large waterfall, Bøsdalafossur, that pours nearly 30 m into the sea. A close view of this magnificent sight is best obtained when flying over the cliffs towards the airport. At the northern end of the lake lies the only inland village in the Faroes – Vatnsoyrar (population 60). It was founded in the 1920s and has a factory, three wholesale shops and a private school.

Vatnsoyrar is by-passed by the main road and on this we shortly reach a road to the left that leads to the airport, originally built by the British during the Second World War. More than 11,000 troops were stationed in Vágar at that time. Sørvágsvatn was also used as a flying-boat base. Even today the planes fly in and out over the lake for the obvious reason that it is flat! There are very few places anywhere in the Faroes that are flat enough to have an airstrip. The runway is quite short – about 1.5 km – and it is difficult to extend it as it lies on a low contour line of the mountain Slættarberg (304 m), meaning 'flat mountain'; and so it follows that there is water at both ends of the flight-path. Until recently only small planes, like the Fokker Friendship, could land here but now modern jets can make a landing using their backthrust. The worst problem is fog because pilots must be able to see both the cliffs they have to pass: either up Sørvágsfjørður between the cliffs on either side, or up over the high rocky barrier that locks Sørvágsvatn in place. Sometimes planes have to circle for hours to seek a gap in the clouds or may have to come back another day. The weather can even exclude all air-traffic for a week. Despite this, nearly 100,000 passengers pass through the airport annually. Luckily, a new hotel nearby can accommodate most stranded passengers. A regular helicopter service to Tórshavn is operative and this also serves the remote villages of Gásadalur, Mykines and Koltur.

Sørvágur

The main road continues downhill to the village of Sørvágur with its 1,000 inhabitants whose brightly coloured houses lie mainly on either side of the bay at the end of a long fjord. The church lies by itself in the centre of the village, next to the inevitable stream that flows through the middle. It was built in 1886 after the previous church was blown down and has, unusually, brown-painted wooden sides and a slate roof plus a white tower. A stone wall surrounds the graveyard around the church and there are large numbers of flowers on the graves. A large green infield can be seen to the south of Sørvágur.

Bøur

Leaving Sørvágur along R 452 on the north side of Sørvágsfjørður you have before you one of the most delightful scenes in the whole of the Faroes. As you gaze across the blue water at the mouth of the fjord, you have an enchanting spectacle of the holms that lie off the coast: the slanting, tall edge of Tindhólmur (262 m) with its spiky peaks that looks like a fairy-tale castle, the curious stacks of the Drangarnir through one of which you can see daylight, and the distant, mysterious island of Mykines.

It is only 4 km to the old village of Bøur. The road clings close to the contours of the mountain and is well above the sea. The village of Bøur has only a score of old turf-roofed houses as well as a few modern dwellings, also with turf roofs, that were put up after the road was built. The wooden church (1865) has tarred wooden walls, a grey slate roof and a white tower, and is next to a stream at the end of the village. This is a quite delightful setting.

The road continues for 2 km past the village and comes to a stop at Rógvukollur (523 m), since it is planned to drive a tunnel through the mountain to Gásadalur, another 2 km distant – the last village not to be linked to the road network. This road ends in a kettle-valley, while a path continues over the hills to Gásadalur, rising up to 500 m before descending on the other side.

There are three ways of getting to the small village of Gásadalur (population 20) which stands 300 ft above vertical cliffs: by walking over the hills, by boat or by helicopter. The hamlet consists of a handful of houses perched high above the steep cliffs at the bottom of a large cirque between Heinanøv (613 m) to the north and Knúkarnir (414 m) to the south. The church is from 1865 and has black walls, with a slate roof and white tower. A path leads sharply downwards to a simple quay among the skerries.

Slættanes was the northernmost village on Vágar, at the mouth of Vestmannasund, between Vágar and Streymoy, and could be reached by a path from Gásadalur, as well as from other places. It was abandoned in the 1960s but the houses are still there.

Mykines

This island is just 10.28 sq. km in area and has only 30 permanent inhabitants. It is 7 km from east to west and not more than 2 km across. The highest point is Knúkur (560 m) and most of the coast is steep and inaccessible. The westernmost point of the island and also of the Faroes, Mykineshólmur, is separated from the main island by a 35-m fissure over which hangs a small suspension bridge. The holm is 133 m high, rich in bird life, and has the only gannetry in the Faroes. The sheep fed on the guano-fed grass wax very fat and are known as 'oxen'. The inhabitants still go fowling since this is one of the best bird islands in the Faroes.

Access to the island by sea has always been problematical because of difficult landing conditions, and the island can be cut off for weeks. However, the helicopter service that links Mykines, Gásadalur and Sørvágur is a little more reliable, though even this can be uncertain in bad weather. At one time peat was cut and coal was mined ·here; today it is more convenient to import coal by helicopter!

TRAIL T: SØRVÁGUR TO MYKINES

From Sørvágur harbour the small ferry boat *Súlan* (the Gannet), makes the hour-long journey to Mykines. The boat has to be small because of difficult landing conditions at Mykines and this means that tickets should be booked well in advance to be sure of a place. You can board only if your name is on the passenger list, but if the weather is bad the sailing is cancelled. You need to be quite agile to undertake this journey since it may be necessary to jump on and off the boat or scramble up the quay-wall, because of the ever-changing tides.

The boat sails up Sørvágsfjørður, keeping to the southern

bank which gives a good sight of the Bøur road, on the opposite bank, as it undulates along the cliffside. We pass by the Drangarnir stacks and sail past Tindhólmur (262 m), a spectacular sight at close quarters as it rises steeply out of the sea with its series of spiky columns, but then the land falls away to grassy fields on the western side. Behind us are the vertical cliffs of the western tip of Vágar on which sea birds make their nests along the ledges. Next we pass the small islet of Gáshólmur and head for the southern coast of Mykines. It is now possible to see over to the remote village of Gásadalur on Vágar.

Because of the strong currents, the ferry has to sail right alongside the steep southern coast of Mykines before reaching the small village of that name, at the western end of the island. Along these cliffs, the many ledges are full of nesting sea birds, the commonest of which is the puffin.

At last the village of Mykines can be seen high up in a sloping valley covered in bright green grass. The boat enters an inlet, in which there is just enough room for the boat to turn round and tie up at the quayside. Facing you is a steep set of 135 concrete steps leading to the lower end of the village.

Mykines is an attractive village with a surprising number of houses considering that it has only 30 permanent inhabitants. Many of the houses have become holiday homes in the summer. On the left is a smelly oil-fired generator for the electricity supply, while on the right is the helipad. A number of the old-fashioned houses have turf roofs, as do some more modern houses, mainly red in colour, from the 1920s and later. The church (1879) is set above the village and is of white concrete with a turf roof and a white spire; it has windows on only the south side. Around the church is a stone wall within which grows a large amount of angelica. A stream flows down the centre of the village with rows of houses on either side.

A large infield lies above the village with many stone-walled fields. At the very edge of the northern part of the infield is an imposing fissure in the rocks where the sides plunge hundreds of metres vertically into the sea. Here, several layers of disintegrating brown tuff are found at 10-m intervals all the way down. Sea birds like to nest on the ledges formed by the erosion of the softer rock.

At the opposite end of the village, to the south-west, a path leads to the end of the island. First, you climb to the top of the hill, above the village, and go along the edge, through the puffin breeding grounds, before descending to the narrow iron suspension bridge that spans the sound separating the main island from Mykineshólmur. It is just another half mile to the end where there is a lighthouse. This is the one place in the Faroes where gannets (*Súlan*) breed. It is a must for bird-watchers for Mykines is renowned as 'The Bird Island'.

18 Sandoy, Skúvoy, Stóra Dímun and Lítla Dímun

Sandoy

'Sand Island' is considered to be the most fertile island in the Faroes. Its area is 112.10 sq. km and it is 23 km long from north-west to south-east, while at its broadest it is 14 km wide; it has a population of almost 1,700. Comparatively speaking Sandoy is quite flat. The highest peak in the middle of the island is Tindur (479 m) but most of the coastline is craggy and inaccessible except where the five main villages are located. It is separated from Hestur and Streymoy by the broad Skopunarfjørður, and from Skúvoy to the south by Skúvoyarfjørður. Two valleys separate the island into three parts: one from Skopun to Sandur and the other from Sandur to Húsavík. A number of lakes are found in these two valleys which are rich in fish.

At the northern tip of the island is a holm, Trøllhøvdi (the Troll's Head), which belongs to the Crown-farmer over at Kirkjubøur, who was keen to exploit this ideal bird-cliff, 166 m high. Indeed, most of the cliffs on Sandoy are good places for fowling. At the farthest eastern coastal edge stands the imposing Skálhøvdi (202 m) that drops straight down into the sea and can be clearly seen both from land and sea.

TRAIL U: TÓRSHAVN TO DALUR VIA SKOPUN

A small car ferry *Tróndur* (ironically named after the pagan chief from Gøta who raided the neighbouring island of Skúvoy and caused the death of the Christian hero Sigmundur) leaves Tórshavn frequently on its journey to Skopun. It can carry only a dozen cars, but a larger vessel cannot be put into service because the entrance to Skopun harbour has to be narrow to protect it against the strong currents in the sound. Attempts over the years have not solved the problems of providing an adequate harbour for this exposed north-easterly place. Despite the fact that Sandoy is relatively low-lying and has rich agricultural land, the island is mainly surrounded by vertical cliffs.

Skopun

Skopun village is relatively young, being founded in 1833, and is placed in the outfield belonging to Sandur village and hence has no infield of its own. From its humble beginnings, as a mere landing stage for the village boat to Kirkjubøur opposite, it has grown into a compact village of 600 people who derive their livelihood mainly from fishing. A modern fish factory lies by the harbour. The church (1897) is made of whitewashed stone and has a red corrugated iron roof.

The village is quite compact with houses on either side of the stream that flows through the middle, while many new houses are found up at the west end. Here we find a helipad and a large rough-hewn standing stone, a memorial to those lost at sea designed by Janus Kamban in 1954. A small bumpy road goes west through the village to a cultivated area of ground.

Roads on Sandoy were the very first ones to be built in the Faroes. In the 1920s, when the fishing became economically problematical, people were given relief-aid if they worked on the roads. Today the roads have all been upgraded and the new R 30 up the cliffside from Skopun gives a good overview of the harbour. To really appreciate the old road and its difficult construction, using manual labour, go south past the church and along its windy and undulating course until you eventually join the modern R 30, after a kilometre or so, on a level part of the valley.

Sandur

R 30 from Skopun climbs up to a level plain with two small lakes on it: Norðara Hálsavatn and Heimara Hálsavatn. By the side of the first lake is a delightful little turf-roofed house that was a gift to a former artist. A little further on, a track to the left climbs up the side of the mountain Knúkur (367 m) and makes its way over to the northern coast. From this track there is a superb vista down the green valley to the delightful village of Sandur whose houses lie in an almost straight line down to the sea. From up here you can see that the village is basically on a peninsula, with the large lake Sandsvatn on the left and Gróthúsvatn on the right, a fact that is not so obvious when in Sandur itself. North of Sandsvatn is the new central school that serves the entire island for secondary education. It was deliberately placed outside the village to make the point that the school belonged to Sandoy and not to Sandur.

The village of Sandur, despite its apparent contiguity, is made up of several hamlets that have grown together, except for the hamlet of í Troðum, on the other side of Sandsvatn, where four Crown-farmers live and have their infields. The population is 640 and is thus the largest village on the island. The name derives from the golden sand dunes at the end of the bay, the only such example in the whole of the Faroes. It is said that the dunes built up after a boat pursuing pilot whales was wrecked and sank in the bay; it is supposed to be still there under the sand. The marram grass that binds the dunes together was introduced by a doctor who wanted to create a football pitch for the young people. Most villages have football teams and competition is fierce.

The church (1839) is by the shore and is the traditional type with black wooden walls, a turf roof and white spire. It has a finely carved screen and the inside is of scrubbed pine. According to archaeological excavations, five churches have been built here and they stem back to the very introduction of Christianity. In a grave dug up in 1863, they discovered 98 silver coins in a solidified clump, of which 43 were German, 24 Anglo-Saxon, 18 Norwegian and 4 Danish, all dating from AD 1070–80. It is thought that these coins came from under the altar of the old church which was in a different place from the present one. More recent excavations outside the present graveyard have revealed Viking graves in the sand. Reports on such archaeological excavations are regularly reported in *Mondul*, the journal issued by the Faroese Prehistory Office.

The hamlet of í Troðum lies under the crags of Sandaskorar (441 m) over which flows a waterfall into Sandsvatn. In windy weather this water is blown back up over the mountainside as spray. The modern harbour is quite extensive and serves the fish factory there. Most of the recent housing has been built along the new road to the harbour that bypasses the older houses. In the middle of the village is a cluster of traditional houses and one of these is called *í Koytu*. This house has been designated as a potential folk museum; the central part of the building is believed to date back to the mid-sixteenth century. If the contents are preserved this could well become the best folk museum in the Faroes.

Most houses in Sandur date from the 1920s, as can be seen from their concrete foundations and brightly painted corrugated iron walls and roofs. A road round Sandsvatn to the north through í Troðum goes past some more old houses but, further along under the mountainside, are some modern timber houses.

A small road to the west, past Gróthúsvatn and Grótvík, leads to a little bay at Søltuvík, 5 km distant. This is a quite delightful trip on a fine evening, for Mykines and its flashing lighthouse can be seen and also Tindhólmur and Vágar in the distance. From here, Tróllhøvdi at the tip of Sandoy is also visible. This bay was never settled because of the innumerable underwater skerries and reefs on which boats have constantly been wrecked.

Skálavík

R 30 out of Sandur goes to Skálavík on the east coast. To the right, R 37 to Skarvanes, 5 km away, passes between two lakes, Lítlavatn and Stóravatn, that are good for angling. On the right are a couple of old houses at Djúpidalur and, 2 km later, we come to Skarvanes, perched high above the precipitous cliffs that line this coast. It has just half a dozen houses and only six people. The fate of many such small hamlets is to be deserted by the young, leaving behind an ageing population. From here we have a direct view across the sound to Skúvoy and its village, besides seeing the Dímunar islands with Suðeroy behind.

Returning to R 30 and continuing south-west, above the small lake, R 35 leads to Húsavík and Dalur to the right, but we continue to Skálavík through the valley between Pætursfjall (446 m) to the north and Vestfelli (396 m) to the south. Eventually the road swings round above the village and Skálavík (population 230) is in full view. It lies in a valley with the same mountain range to the north but Heidarfjall (226 m) and Skálhøvdi (202 m) to the south. The main road runs right down the middle of the village to the small harbour but minor roads go along either side up the valley sides. It has quite a large infield and here, also, is the largest Crown-farm in the island and one of the biggest in all the Faroes: the Dalsgarður farm.

Skálavík church (1891) lies by itself in the centre of the infield, which is unusual since most churches are by the shore. There used to be a small church above the small harbour but this was destroyed in a storm. The current building is of white stone with a turf roof and the interior has been entirely refurbished with new stained-wooden pews, while the walls and ceiling are covered with new wooden panels that give a lovely warm feeling. In the graveyard around the church the graves are all neatly numbered, while a register of the names of the dead is kept in the vestry.

Some early twentieth-century style houses remain, but much of the housing is of modern wooden construction. Its new prosperity is based on fishing that is mainly undertaken from other villages, and from Tórshavn in particular.

Húsavík

R 35 to this village branches off R 30 to the right before Skálavík and goes through a broad green valley between the mountains. The actual village of Húsavík (population 115) lies on a sandy bay between Heidafjallur (266 m) to the north and Stórafjallur (396 m) to the south. The two halves of the village lie on either side of the infield. It has a small harbour and some boathouses nearby.

Húsavík has quite a large number of traditional houses with turf roofs near to the church which itself dates from 1863. The latter has whitewashed stone walls and a turf roof while the graves are carefully numbered in the graveyard. Nearby are the ruins of the large farm *Heimi á Garði* that belonged to the Lady of Húsavík in the fifteenth century. She was a Norwegian who also owned properties in Shetland and was the richest person in the Faroes of her time, as the impressive ruins of her farm still show.

Near to the church is an old house, *á Breyt*, built in the traditional style with tarred wooden walls and turf roof. It is preserved as a folk museum and is always open. It was lived in until recently, but today there are only a few token objects left since there is no permanent custodian. On the other side of the used infield is another group of houses.

One of the few villages to have preserved its charm, Húsavík is well worth a visit.

Dalur

R 35 actually by-passes the village of Húsavík and climbs up the side of Stórafjall (396 m). This single-track road clings to the precipitous cliffs around a blunted promontory before it swings round and begins a steep descent to the village of Dalur. The small and sharply sloping valley between Stórafjall and Skúvoyarfjall (349 m) contains the 30-odd houses gathered together in a clump at the bottom, where 70 people live. Along the steep valley sides, old cultivation terraces can be clearly seen.

A number of houses are quite old, with stone foundations and turf roofs, while there are just a few modern houses. The little white wooden church (1957) with a green roof lies quite apart from the other houses, near a sandy beach and on the other side of the stream that flows down the centre of the village.

Just before entering the village, across the stream, a road bends sharply to the right and up the valley. This rough road zigzags up the hillside giving excellent views of the tiny village below. The road continues past Skúvoyarfjall (349 m) and stops not far from the bird-cliffs of Skorin. It was built during the war for defence purposes and the Dalur men had to complete so many metres each, every year. At the bottom of these near-vertical cliffs is a 3-km long ledge where the people of Dalur graze some of their sheep on rich guano-fed grass. These fat sheep then have to be hauled up with a hoist. Fowling still continues along the rich bird-cliffs of Sandoy and as many as 1,000 puffins can be caught in a single day, by just one fowler.

From this high point can be seen all the islands to the south – Skúvoy, Dímunar and the whole length of Suðeroy – and so it was a good look-out point for defence purposes. Below, hundreds of puffins fly in great anti-clockwise circles, coming parallel to the coast, where the fowlers wait for them in the summer.

Skúvoy

'Great Skua Island' well describes the island of Skúvoy, which is 10 sq. km in area and has a population of 90 people. This was the place where John Buchan set his thrilling novel *The Island of Sheep*. It is 5 km long and 3 km wide. The village is on the middle of the east coast where a valley slopes down to the sea. The island is separated from Sandoy by Skúvoyarfjørður and from Stóra Dímun by Dímunarfjørður. The west coast is extremely steep and has excellent bird-cliffs near the highest peak, Knútur. Traditional fowling and egg collecting are still practised.

TRAIL V: TO SKÚVOY

Only two ways of getting to the island of Skúvoy are possible: by helicopter from Tórshavn or from Froðba on Suðuroy, or by boat from Sandur. The cheapest way, of course, is to take the small ferry boat *Sildberin* (the Fish-bearer which refers to a puffin bringing small herring to its young). Amusingly enough, the boat brings a load of people from Skúvoy to work in the fish factory in Sandur.

The small village on Skúvoy lies on the east coast, in the only valley on the island, between outliers of the highest mountain, Knútur (392 m), to the west and Snatin (300 m) to the south-west. The houses are perched some 50 m above the shoreline; indeed, some 90-odd steps (cf. Mykines) lead up from the small harbour to the first houses on this sloping site. A slipway to haul the boats up to the boathouses at the top is now disused since a new road has been built up to the village. To the north, along the coast, is another landing place that is used if the wind is unfavourable for landing at the main harbour.

Skúvoy church (1937) lies by itself near a fissure on the other side of the stream that goes through the village. It is made of white cement and has a red plastic roof. A teacher who taught both here and at Dalur was the moving force in getting these two churches built. A helipad is next to the church.

About 300 yd south of the church, almost at the end of the infield, is the old graveyard of í Olansgarði where the saga hero Sigmundur Brestirson is supposed to be buried. At the top of the graveyard there is a small grave with a stone bearing a cross that indicates his grave. A similar engraved stone, nearby, was sent to the National Museum in Copenhagen in 1842. It is said that victims of the Black Death, c. 1350, were buried here and people were too frightened to use the graveyard again, but, by 1917, they needed to re-use it. They found remains of a coffin, the foundations of what might have been the church that Sigmundur was supposed to have built here, as well as stones engraved with Latin crosses and wheel-crosses that are similar in design to Irish crosses – so Irish monks might have been here!

Sigmundur Brestirson is famed for having tried to introduce Christianity into the Faroes in AD 997, but was opposed by his pagan arch-enemy, Tróndur úr Gøta. In 1005, Tróndur made a surprise attack on Sigmundur at his home on Skúvoy, but the latter escaped over the hills and swam with two companions to Suðuroy. Only Sigmundur reached the shore at Sandvík where he was murdered by Torgrímur the Evil, for the sake of his gold ring.

The 25 houses in Skúvoy are built quite closely together,

overlooking the harbour, and contain 90 people. They are not allowed to keep cats since they attack the birds, but no rats or mice live on Skúvoy. Puffins are caught on the north side of the island opposite to Sandur, while fulmar eggs are also collected from the steep bird-cliffs on the west side. One or two tracks go along the infields. They do not go anywhere of special interest to the visitor but you can always observe the sloping hillsides that provide hay for the sheep. The people have no local peat and in the olden days they had to fetch it from the boggy area around Stóravatn on Sandoy.

Stóra Dímun

Seven km south of Sandoy lies the almost impregnable island of Stóra Dímun, 2.65 sq. km area. It is separated from Skúvoy by Dímunarfjørður. From north-west to south-east it is 3 km long, and barely 1 km across. The highest point is Høgoyggi (396 m) which lies to the north. The surrounding cliffs are seldom lower than 100 m and most of them are bird-cliffs. A sloping area to the south leads to a single farm, as well as the vitally necessary helipad.

TRAIL W: TO STÓRA DÍMUN

The only way to reach Stóra Dímun nowadays is by helicopter from Tórshavn or Froðba. The reason is that the island has 100-m cliffs all around and has only one landing place, whence steps hewn into the rockface are used to climb up the cliffs with the aid of a steel cable. In any case it is very rare that the wind and tide are just right to be able to pull up alongside this small quay. In 1874 the minister who was visiting the island slipped on this perilous path and fell to his death, so people are discouraged from using it.

A single farm has been in constant occupation here since Viking times until quite recently, when it was temporarily abandoned in the winter because of the poor landing facilities. However, with the helicopter service the present young farmer has come back and settled here permanently with his family. An advantage of this air service is that teachers can be flown in to teach the younger children; this peripatetic educational facility is also shared with the two other remote villages of Gásadalur and Mykines.

Normally the helicopter flies right over Sandoy and touches down in Skúvoy before going on to Stóra Dímun, but if there is low cloud it skims over the fjords and avoids the mountains. The helipad on Stóra Dímun is on the south side, next to the farm, and to reach this sloping infield the plane flies close to the eastern cliffs and then lifts up and over them before circling and touching down.

Most of the island is mountainous and the highest point is Høgoyggi in the north, although the ground slopes away southwards forming a high pasture. The brown timber-clad farmhouse itself is quite large with many outbuildings, while almost all around the main building there is a massive, high stone wall that acts as a windshield, except for the southern aspect. From here, neighbouring Lítla Dímun and Suðuroy are plainly visible.

Near the farmhouse are the ruins of a church put up in 1873 but which fell into disuse in 1923. The altar piece was a gift of a former Crown-farmer and is now in the living-room. At one time the local minister from Sandoy used to come twice a summer to hold services, but this is no longer the case.

The island has a rich bird life and so the farmer catches both puffins and guillemots, besides gathering birds' eggs, for this is a traditional way of ekeing out the winter food supplies. At present they have a few dairy cows and some 450 breeding ewes on these rich sloping pastures.

Lítla Dímun

This 0.82-sq. km conical island of Lítla Dímun rises to a height of 413 m and is quite inaccessible, except to the utterly determined, hence it is uninhabited except for summer sheep. It is 5 km south of Stóra Dímun and 13 km east of the village of Hvalba on Suðeroy, to whom it belongs, and who use it to graze sheep. Once it had indigenous wild Faroese sheep that resembled the St Kilda strain, but these sheep were eradicated by the farmers. This is a good place for fowling but it is a very difficult undertaking.

19 Suðuroy

With 166 sq. km, Suðuroy, 'The South Island', is the fourth largest island in the Faroes and has a population of 5,900. It is 32 km from Múlin in the north to Akraberg in the south and is 13 km broad at its widest. The coastline is irregular and has three major eastern inlets, Hvalbiarfjørður, Trongisvágsfjørður and Vágsfjørður, that provide good anchorage for the villages that give their names to these fjords.

All the villages except Fámjin are on the eastern coast because the west is extremely rugged. The highest peak is Gluggarnir (610 m) to the south-west of Tvøroyri. The next highest mountain is Borgarknappur (574 m), south of the western village of Fámjin. Many lakes exist in the valley between í Botni on the west (which has a hydro-electricity plant) and the village of Hov on the east. Coal has been mined in the valley that leads from Tvøroyri to Hvalba in the north, and some mines are still worked.

TRAIL X: TÓRSHAVN TO AKRABERG VIA VÁGUR

The best way to see Suðuroy (apart from taking a helicopter) is to catch one of the larger car-ferries from Tórshavn, either *Smyril* (the Merlin) or her sister ship *Teistin* (the Black Guillemot). The normally smooth ride takes you past the coast of Sandoy, where all the villages can be seen in turn: Skopun at the northern end, and then in quick succession Skálavík, Húsavík and Dalur, before looking up Skúvoyarfjørður towards Skarvanes and Sandur on the south coast, while at the same time Skúvoy village can be seen on its own little island.

Next we sail past the fortress-like island of Stóra Dímun with its single farm, and its smaller companion, uninhabited Lítla Dímun. The mountains in the southern half of Suðuroy are clearly visible at this point in the journey. To the west is the village of Sandvík at the northern end of the island while a little to the south is the village of Hvalba. The vessel then passes by Froðba village at the mouth of Trongisvágsfjørður, then the village of Hov in its little bay before entering Vágsfjørður. On the north side of this fjord is Porkeri village whose white houses are picked out against the sloping green hills as you gaze over the bluish water. To the south is the narrow Lopransfjørður with the village of Lopra at its end. We eventually arrive at Vágur, the largest single village in Suðuroy (population 1,700). Indeed, Vágur is second only to Klaksvík in size, as a village, but it is the local administrative unit, the *kommune*, that is the really decisive political unit and this pushes Vágur into fifth place, behind Froðba *kommune* with its 2,100 inhabitants in north Suðuroy.

For most of the latter part of this two-hour journey you can look back and see both Dímunar and Skúvoy with little white cloud-caps over them, as well over Sandoy.

Vágur

Vágur village is mainly set out in almost parallel rows on the north side of the fjord, under the sloping hillsides. The very large church stands out prominently in the middle of the village. It was built between 1927–39 when the village, which had been one of the most important fishing ports in the Faroes, suffered during the world recession of the 1920s. This may account for the long time it took to complete this church. It is made of grey concrete with a green roof and a huge tower and was the first church since the Reformation ever to have been consecrated by a bishop. This building is in the Gothic style and is reminiscent more of a *Danish* church than anything else.

It is said that the oldest church in Vágur, came drifting from Norway, all ready to be erected! A mourning widow, whose husband was lost at sea, had this church made, bundled up and thrown into the sea with the wish that it would land where it would be most needed. This gift offering was accompanied by a healing stone that could cure all known ills, but the latter was later thrown into the sea as being witchcraft. However, the holy reputation of the church demanded that it ought to receive votive gifts and this has continued ever since, so Vágur has, in consequence, the richest collection of such votive objects in all the Faroes. Outside the church door is a bronze statue of Dean Dahl, who laid the foundation stone of the church, and who was born in Vágur. He was famous as a translator of Biblical texts into Faroese and is regarded as a great patriot.

Vágur has an excellent, protected harbour, a large fish processing plant, many shops and offices, and also a hotel. At the end of the bay there is a lake on the isthmus, while further west is an old landing place that was sometimes used in emergencies.

Round the bay, at the bottom of the fjord, stand many boathouses and also an unmarked road to the south that takes off sharply to the right, up an exceedingly windy and steep climb to the viewpoint of Skúvanøs, that lies 203 m above perpendicular cliffs on the west coast. Here are some stupendous views, both north and south, of the jagged bird-cliffs which are sheer vertical cliffs bright with green vegetation, as well as numerous stacks and skerries, besides thousands of sea birds. It is even possible to see the skerries that lie far off Sumba, called Flesjarnar. The view on returning down to Vágur is equally rewarding.

South of Vágur is R 21 to Sumba. It runs along the side of the fjord and at the point called Núpur the road swings along Lopransfjørður where you can catch sight of the imposing heights of Spáafelli (458 m) to the south-west. The little villages on the northern side of the fjord can be seen before we come to Lopra at the head of its bay.

Lopra (population 100) was once a whaling station and the rusting buildings are still there. Today there is a fish farm and some 30 houses. Test-drilling for gas deposits, undertaken here in 1983, proved positive but the exact results have not yet been disclosed. Up the fjord the small village of Nes, on Vágsfjørður, is visible on the other shore.

R 218 runs round the fjord to Leiti under the steep slopes of Siglifelli (359 m) where a combined church and school, made of yellow concrete with a red roof (1957), serves both Lopra and Akrar (population 50). The latter village is at the end of the road and has a number of small houses from earlier this century. We get a good view right across Vágsfjørður to some of the villages on the north side.

Returning, past Lopra, on R 21 we come to the entrance of a projected tunnel through the mountains to the village of Sumba that avoids the tortuously steep climb up over the mountains. However, to go through this tunnel would be to deny yourself some fascinating views from the top.

After climbing and negotiating half a dozen hairpin bends, we come to a left-hand fork leading down R 217, which is also steep and twisty, to the settlement at Víkarbyrgi that consists of a couple of houses. On the other side of the stream is the single farm of Hamrarbyrgi. A fish farm is here and nothing much else in this steep little valley. The medieval inhabitants all died of the Black Death and the village was abandoned ever afterwards.

Back up on top again, we continue along R 21 to wriggle up Hólmsskorafjallur towards Spáafelli (458 m) and the radio mast where a pull off is situated at a place called Hestur. This is just above Beinisvørd (469 m) and other vertical cliffs, *but beware* (as the notice of a falling man warns), the grassy edges are often undermined and can give way. The cliffs and the skerries are quite stupendous to look at. It is possible to see the northern end of Suðuroy and even as far away as Eysturoy, 40 miles to the north. The southernmost holm in the Faroes, Sumbiasteinur, lying 6 miles away to the south-east, can also be discerned from here.

R 21 now continues down along the side of the mountain and, with a couple of sharp bends, we come above the extremely colourful village of Sumba (population 380) with its large infield. The village contains houses from the first half of the century and they line the shore, up to the harbour, at the west end. The church (1887) is made of white painted stone and has a red roof. A few sheep are set out on the holm that lies offshore to fatten there, because the guano produces rich grass for fodder.

We reach the southern tip of Suðuroy by going along the small R 212 to the lighthouse at Akraberg, perched on the edge of the near-vertical promontory with just a few houses and a radio transmitter. From here, looking towards Sumbiarsteinur, whirlpools can be seen constantly forming out to sea. Equally interesting views may be had all the way back along R 21 to Vágur.

TRAIL Y: VÁGUR TO FROÐBA

Leaving Vágur and taking R 20 along Vágsfjørður we shortly come to the point that gives the hamlet of Nes its name and which has just half a dozen houses besides a small landing stage.

R 20 bypasses the village of Porkeri (population 370) a little further on. It lies around a series of inlets or bays in a valley with a large infield below the ridge of Kambur (205 m) on the east coast and has a fairly large harbour with boathouses nearby. The church (1847) is at the head of one of the small bays and is of the traditional type with tarred wooden walls and a turf roof. It has a finely carved screen and a well-made stone wall around the graveyard.

The layout of the streets is unusual, since they are not in a line facing the shore but are at different angles. Up the northern slopes is a modern school building painted red, with a turf roof. On the outskirts is a large stone obelisk (1966) to the 65 people who died at sea over the last 150 years.

Hov

R 20 now climbs up the Kambur ridge and down the other side from where the village of Hov (population 160) in its wide bay can be seen. The houses are spread in two rows alongside the northern edge of the bay, below the steep sides of the mountain Kolheyggjur (414 m), and from where a vast kettle-valley stretches all the way back, westwards, to the peaks of Borgaknappur (574 m).

Hov church lies in the middle of the village. It was built originally in 1862 for Vágur, but when a new church was completed in Vágur their old church was removed to Hov in 1942 and rebuilt in 1943. The wooden church is black with a turf roof and has a peculiar two-tiered tower.

Most of the houses on the northern part of the road are from the first half of the century, but some on the southern side are modern. There is a small harbour with an early merchant's warehouse and some ruinous boat sheds. There is a fish farm.

The name 'Hov' refers to a heathen Viking temple that, allegedly, stood here. The place is famous in the sagas for being the farm of Havgrímur or Torgrímur the Evil, who murdered Sigmundur Brestirson. Up the hillside, in the infield, is a burial mound reputed to be that of Havgrímur.

Climbing back up to R 20 and stopping at the first hairpin bend, a track runs westwards to a large lake, Vatnsnes, as well as many smaller ones. This is not really a driving road. In the boggy ground, above the road, can be seen the line of cairns that mark the path up the mountain to the various neighbouring villages before there were roads. This walk is not to be recommended without local guides.

R 20 now goes along the mountainside above Hov, while on the left are vertical basalt columns, made familiar to the British by Fingal's Cave in Scotland and the Giant's Causeway in Ireland. The road now swings north around the headland, high above the sea. From this vantage point we have a superb view of Lítla Dímun in the distance, as well as being able to see right up Trongisvágsfjørður and the houses of Tvøroyri, and the steep cliffs of Froðbiarnípa (324 m) at the eastern end of the fjord.

The road now begins its way down to Øravík (population 60) and drops 200 m in the process. Eventually, we arrive at the small village of Øravík that lies by the water with a pebble beach and a small harbour, under the slopes of Oyrnafjallur (443 m). A score of oldish houses, a new hotel and a modern chapel (1966) are found here. The last building is of black wooden construction and has a large red corrugated iron roof, but, as there is no tower, it looks like an enormous boat shed with windows. Only a cross beneath the gable indicates its purpose. There are fish farms in the bay. In the middle of the village a road goes left to Fámjin village.

R 25 to Fámjin snakes its way up the hill, until it reaches the pass between Fjallið Mikla (462 m) that dominates the skyline above Øravík, and Nónfjall (430 m) to the south. We come to a vast and impressive cirque, with several lakes in it, that lies back to back to the even larger cirque that dominates the valley at Hov. The road then spirals down, affording fascinating views over the almost perpendicular west coastline.

Fámjin

Fámjin (population 130) is a picturesque village and the only one on the west coast of Suðuroy, besides being the most isolated one before the road was built. R 25 almost reaches the coast but a sharp right turn takes it down into the village, with its large infield. Three clusters of houses encircle the bay along the road that leads to the church.

It has a pebble beach and a harbour at the northern end of the village bay with boathouses. A fish farm produces smolt, using the water from the lake Kirkjuvatn, above the village. It is far too exposed here to have ring-nets in the bay, so the small fish are sold elsewhere, for further growth. A waterfall from the lake, behind the church, accounts for the name of the lake.

The church (1876) is of whitewashed stone and has a grey slate roof. The inside is also white but the valved ceiling is blue. The chief point of interest here is the first Faroese flag, designed by three Faroese students in Copenhagen in 1919. The credit for the flag, which is in a case hanging on the inside wall to the left, is given to Jens Oliver Lisberg who is buried just outside the church. In the porch is a small rune stone that has Latin engraved on it as well. The runes date from after the Reformation and read 'D.P.S.F.', which is also repeated in Latin. This was probably a gravestone but it is curious that runes were still being used so late as the seventeenth century.

Returning back along R 25 to Øravík, we then continue, left, on R 20 to Tvøroyri. By going along the shore line at the bay end of Trongisvágsfjørður, we get a complete view of the village stretching along the northern shore, below a long mountain ridge.

Tvøroyri

Tvøroyri is the largest of the three villages that form a continuous settlement, on the northern coast of the fjord, from Trongisvágur at the head of the bay to the village of Froðba at the other end. Their total population is 2,100 which makes them the largest *kommune* in Suðuroy, and the fourth biggest in the Faroes. The rapid growth in population over the last century was due to the setting-up here of an out-station of the Royal Monopoly, just before its abolition in 1856. The private merchants quickly developed a thriving fishing industry here, after the initial success of sloop fishing had been proved. Suðuroy, with its many fine, sheltered fjords became the leading place in the Faroes, since it was conveniently close to the fishing grounds. However, after the world recession in the 1920s the island stagnated, and the lead was taken over by Klaksvík and Tórshavn in the further development of new fishing and financial opportunities, to the north of this once-favoured island.

A small settlement on the southern shore of the fjord is a dispersed one lying under Oyrnafjall (443 m) and consists of just two hamlets: Punthaven and Liðin. Here is a salt-bunker that was bombed during the war but was rebuilt later. This is the quayside from where the Tórshavn ferry departs.

At the end of the bay, at Trongisvágur, R 29 runs westwards to Hvalba. The main settlement of Tvøroyri is built up in layers, along and above the eastward-going R 20. In the centre is a large quay and fish processing plant, as well as the premises of the old established timber-merchant company of Richard B. Thomsen. A director of this company wrote many lively accounts, in the form of novels, about conditions here at the turn of the century.

Above the harbour is a hotel, and nearby is the church (1908) of most unusual proportions. It looks *Norwegian in style* and the timber was actually shaped in Norway. The church was a gift from the rich merchant family of Mortensen who were the founders of Tvøroyri's prosperity. This large, all-wooden construction can hold 600 worshippers. The church is painted cream, has a red corrugated iron roof and occupies a very commanding position over the village. It is an amusing reflection that the rival fishing village of Vágur has a large *Danish-style church*. We have the *exact* parallel in the island of Vágar between the rival villages of Sandavágur and Miðvágur with their large and atypical churches.

A small plantation is found above the hospital and many houses have flourishing trees and bushes in their own gardens: fir and plane trees, whitebeam and willow, with lots of flowering currants. Tvøroyri has a very old-fashioned air about it, the shops are not modern and many are still in the basements of houses, which was once common practice.

A few kilometres eastwards from the church, on R 27, is the small village of Froðba which gave its name to the whole parish, since a church had been here ever since the Middle Ages. A wooden church with a turf roof was erected here in 1840 but then moved to Tvøroyri in 1856 at the end of the Royal Monopoly period. There it served the growing population until a new church was built in 1907, when the old church was moved on to the village of Sandvík.

Froðba village comprises many small houses dispersed along a network of short roads above a little harbour, while nearby is a helipad with direct flights to Stóra Dímun and to Tórshavn. At the end of the main road, R 27, in a bend, is an old water mill in the dip. It is possible to continue, by road, right to the coast at Skarvatangi where, high over the sea, the vertical basalt cliffs of Nakkur (324 m) to the north can be seen, as well as across the fjord to the southern cliffs.

TRAIL Z: TVØROYRI TO SANDVÍK

R 29 runs westward through the large infield at Trongisvágur and, after 3 km, an old road on the left (opposite a quarry) winds its way up to an old coal mine at Rangnabotnur (350 m). The main road, however, does a double swing before entering the first of two tunnels built in 1963, 1.4 km long and single-track. You emerge at the head of a broad, flat valley through which the river Dalsá meanders to a delta in Hvalbiarfjørður. The village of Hvalba lies straight ahead. On both sides of the valley are coal mines: those to the left, along R 29 under Prestfjall (472 m), are disused, but on the other side, under Hvalbiarfjall, they are still operational. The coal is not of high quality and, although important in the last war, it is of little significance today.

Hvalba

The road proceeds down the mountainside to the village of Hvalba that is rather dispersed around a sandy bay and stands on an isthmus. We come first to the church (1935) with its white cement walls and dark red roof. Some of the church silver was given by the British Government in thanks for rescuing and burying the dead from the trawler *St Bernhard* that was stranded near Hvalba in 1901.

Hvalba has 700 inhabitants who live in a semicircle around a bay which has two harbours: a large one, with a fish factory on the northern side, and a marina further out, with a memorial to those lost at sea between 1890–1960.

A small track goes south of the village towards the west coast, past a small lake, Heygsvatn. It ends above the rocks where some steps lead down a fissure to a boathouse and a landing place, where boats could be hauled up. A good view of the neighbouring mountain of Grímsfjall (327 m) is to be had from here.

Near the church, and off the main road, is another southern road, R 293, that leads to Nes on the east side. It crosses a bridge with a spit to the left and a lagoon to the right. There is a little harbour here between two curved moles that is protected by a tongue of land. Just 20 houses line the road before it ends abruptly; this is directly opposite the tunnel entrance to Sandvík, on the other side of the fjord.

Sandvík

R 29 then curves along the bay at Hvalba, climbs steeply, and then plunges into the mountainside of Skálafjallur (373 m) through the 1.5-km tunnel (built in 1970) and emerges with Sandvík village down before us. The road swings left and curves towards the village in a large sweep across a sandy estuary, through which a river meanders. Although it has a pleasant grey sandy bay, the 40 or so houses in which the 120 villagers live are built on the rocky northern side.

The church (1908) with white wooden walls and a pale green roof was moved here from Tvøroyri when that village got a new church. Just nearby is an old farmhouse in the traditional style with tarred walls and turf roof, that functions as a folk museum.

An old road can be found that climbs westwards near the river Sandvíksá, through agricultural land with many gates to keep in the sheep. This 2-km long road winds its way up the side of the mountain ridge Eggin (360 m) that separates Sandvík from Hvalba, and then suddenly stops. This well-drained road was an attempt to drive a road over the mountain to Hvalba but it became too difficult. However, if we continue to the western edge, on foot, we get a superlative view over to Mykines and Vágar, while looking back there is a picturesque vista of the small village of Sandvík, down in the bay, with Lítla Dímun sticking up out of the sea in the far distance.

V BASIC FACTS

Appendix A

Transport

It is advisable to check with your travel agent, well in advance of any intended journey to the Faroes, as the situation changes from year to year. At the time of writing no direct air link exists between Britain and the Faroes.

CAR FERRIES

Esbjerg, Denmark to Tórshavn

The Danish DFDS Scandinavian Seaways sails from Esbjerg to Tórshavn every Monday in June, July and August. The journey takes 35 hours. The current vessel is the *Winston Churchill* which can take 800 passengers and 180 cars.

Hanstholm, Denmark to Tórshavn

The Faroese Smyril line sails from Hanstholm every Saturday in June, July and August. The journey takes 34 hours. The vessel is the *Norröna* which can take 1080 passengers and 250 cars.

Lerwick, Shetland to Tórshavn

The Faroese Smyril line also sails from Lerwick every Wednesday from June to August. The journey takes 13 hours. The vessel is also the *Norröna*. To take your car it means catching the P & O ferry *St Clair* from Aberdeen to Lerwick on Monday, which makes this an extremely expensive journey altogether, besides having to hang around in Lerwick for 18 hours till the small hours.

Scrabster, Caithness to Tórshavn

The Faroese Government ferry sails from Scrabster to Tórshavn every Saturday from June to August. The journey takes 13 hours. The vessel is the inter-island *Smyril* and has 180 berths and can take 110 cars. As this route is subsidized it means that it can be discontinued without notice. This is the cheapest way to get to the Faroes.

AIR TRAVEL

Copenhagen to Vágar

The Danish airline Danair has daily flights throughout the year but no service is available on Sundays in the winter. The flight time is 2 hours. Because of uncertainty regarding the weather at Vágar airport flights may be delayed both coming and going.

Copenhagen to Vágar

The Faroese airline Atlantic Airways also has daily flights to Vágar.

Reykjavik to Vágar

The Icelandic airline Icelandair has a couple of flights a week to Vágar.

INTERNAL TRAVEL

A comprehensive network of buses and ferries exists which will take you to most places. It is essential to get a timetable from the Information offices in order to plan your journeys. Except for the ferry to Mykines and all helicopter flights, no advance booking is possible. If you take a car then you must queue in good time to be certain of a place since some car ferries are quite small. You should be aware that there are 20,000 motor vehicles in the Faroes today as compared with a mere 3,500 twenty years ago!

It is always possible to hire a car in the Faroes and the rates compare favourably with those in Britain, so this may be an attractive proposition. The absolute maximum speed allowed is 80 km/hr (50 mph) on highways; in built-up areas it is 50 km/hr (30 mph) but it can be reduced to 30 km/hr (20 mph) in small villages. The penalties for exceeding any speed limit by more than 30 km/hr is confiscation of your licence. If you have more than 0.8 per cent of alcohol in your blood when driving the result is a fine and loss of your licence. The police are very strict.

Accommodation

Altogether there are only about 20 hotels and boarding-houses in the Faroes. The total available number of beds is 1,200, but a third of these are in Tórshavn. The prices are what you would expect in Scandinavia. Most hotels have a restaurant.

Just half a dozen youth hostels are to be found in various parts of the Faroes. Camping is not to be recommended because you need the landowners' permission first, while the uncertainties of the weather make it hazardous and only those really capable of handling tents in extreme conditions should attempt it.

It is possible to stay in private accommodation but these facilities are not advertised and so you must ask the Tourist Bureaux in Tórshavn to arrange things.

Meals

While most hotels have restaurants there are only a dozen cafés in the rest of the Faroes outside Tórshavn, so meals can be a problem. Most villages have food shops but you still need the means to cook your food.

The only alcoholic drink served or that can be bought is light beer. It is possible for tourists, though, to purchase strong beer direct from the local brewers after going through certain cumbersome formalities, such as proving you do not owe the government any taxes! Wines and spirits have to be ordered from Denmark and you are rationed to 42 litres of strong beer, 3 litres of wine and 3 litres of spirits for every 30 days of your visit. Of course you can bring with you the usual quantities of duty free: one bottle of spirits and a bottle of wine and two litres of strong beer in long-necked bottles – *canned beer is a prohibited item*. For the curious, one might add that the British Customs also have some odd restrictions, like the fact that you may not import into the UK more than 50 litres of beer from the Faroes nor more than 25 mechanical lighters! One wonders how this last restriction ever arose – is there a black market in lighters? Perhaps this obsolete regulation may be linked with the fact that you cannot bring more than 6 lb of sweets into the Faroes – it must be treading on somebody's monopoly!

General

The above notes indicate the general position for tourists at the time of writing (1990). You should seek as much recent information as possible from your travel agent before setting off to the Faroes, or write direct to the Faroese Tourist Board: Ferðamannamiðstöðin, Skansavegur 1, FR-100 Tórshavn, The Faroe Islands.

Office, shop and bank hours are between 8 to 9 a.m. until 5.30 on weekdays. Most shops close at noon on Saturdays; offices and banks are not open then. Newspaper and sweet kiosks in most villages are open every day from the afternoon until 11 p.m. These kiosks also sell milk, soft drinks, bread and butter, and other basic items.

The weather is quite capricious but rarely cold, though it can be quite windy. The same goes for the North Sea which can be quite choppy. So be prepared!

Appendix B

545	The Irish St Brendan is alleged to have visited the Faroes on his way to Iceland and named them 'the Sheep Islands'.
825	The Irish monk Dicuil wrote a book: *De mensura orbis* (The measurement of the Earth) which mentions many islands, some of which might be the Faroes.
c. 825	Grímur Kamban is the first settler on the Faroes.
930	The first *Alting* assembly is held at Tinganes.
c. 1000	Christianity is acknowledged by the *ting* (*Løgting*) in Tórshavn. Political and religious struggles between the heathen Tróndur úr Gøta and the Christian Sigmundur Brestirson occur.
1030	The Norwegian king, St Olaf, is killed at the battle of Stiklestad on 29 July. Later he becomes the patron saint of the Faroes.
c. 1035	Leif Øssursson, Tróndur's foster son, receives the Faroes as a fiefed province from King Magnus the Good of Norway.
1066	Olaf the Gentle visits the Orkneys and the Faroes.
1080– c. 1540	The Faroes become a bishopric under the Archbishop of Nidaros (now Trondheim), Norway, with the see at Kirkjubøur.
1151	Sverre, later King of Norway, born in the Faroes at Kirkjubøur.
1273	The trade monopoly is instituted. King Magnus the Law-mender promises to send two merchant vessels a year to the Faroes. In the same year the king declared that the Norwegian Gulating Law applied to the Faroes, whereby their independence under their *ting* led by the Lawman ceased and the latter became a royal official.

1280	The Faroes are named for the first time on the Mappa mundi, in Hereford cathedral, and called *Farei* (The sheep island).
1294	The Hansa League merchants are forbidden to trade with the Norwegian dependencies, including the Faroes, but they continue as before.
1298	The Sheep Letter (*Seyðabrævið*), an additional law concerning the use of the land, especially the outfield, is imposed by Duke Håkan Magnusson on 28 June.
c. 1300	The Magnus cathedral is begun in Kirkjubøur but was never completed. Erlend was bishop: 1269–1308.
1302	Hansa merchants are forbidden to trade with the Faroes.
1361	The Hansa merchants receive the same trading-rights as Norwegians, in the dependencies. Stiff competition from the English merchants.
1380	The Faroes and other possessions, together with Norway, are placed under the Danish crown but are still administered as Norwegian provinces.
1468	Christian I, King of Norway and Denmark, pledges Orkney and Shetland as a dowry for his daughter's marriage with James III of Scotland.
1490	The Dutch obtain the same trading rights in Norway and its possessions, as the Hansa merchants.
1500	The Faroes are raided by French, British, Irish and Algerian pirates. The latter are called Turks.
1529	King Fredrik I gives the Faroes, in fiefdom, to two Hamburg merchants, Thomas Koppen and Joachim Wullenweber, for 100 Lübeck marks per year. They also receive an absolute trade monopoly and the right to set taxes.
1536	The Norwegian Council of the Realm is abolished and both the Faroes and Norway are now ruled as part of Denmark.
c. 1540	The Reformation. The Faroes becomes a Protestant diocese. King Christian III immediately confiscates two-thirds of the Church property.
1547	The king hands over the disposition of the confiscated Church lands to his (German) countryman, Thomas Koppen, on certain conditions.
c. 1540–57	Jens Gregersen Riber is made the Christian superintendent (bishop) of the Faroes.
1550	In a Royal Letter of 12 March, the Faroese are given the right to appeal against the Lawman's judgements to the king in his capacity as King of Norway. That the Faroes were not reckoned as a Norwegian province is clear from Christian

IV's Norwegian law, which does not even mention the Faroese *ting* amongst the Norwegian *tings*.

1553   With the death of Thomas Koppen, trade became freer, i.e. the Faroese could then trade with Danish and Norwegian merchants but not with foreigners.

1556–71   The trade monopoly is revived by the king.

1557   The Faroese diocese is abolished and the islands become part of Bergen's see. Heine Jonsson, Magnus Heinason's father, is made the first dean of the Faroes. The remaining third of the Church's property is confiscated by the king.

1571–8   Free trade.

1579   Magnus Heinason obtains trading rights.

1584   A sworn *ting* secretary (sorenskriver) is installed to keep the minutes of the *ting* and assist the members in judicial matters.

1589   Magnus Heinason is beheaded in Copenhagen for treason.

1604   Christian IV's Norwegian Law comes into effect.

1619–62   The Icelandic Company takes hand on both trade monopolies and (until 1655) all the royal income from the Faroes, for a yearly sum of 1,000 rigsdaler.

1632   Additional farms granted to ministers in compensation for their loss.

1655–1709   The Gabel régime. In 1655 Fredrik III guarantees Christoffer Gabel all the income from the Faroes for 1,000 rigsdaler annually. In 1661 this privilege is extended to him and his son Fredrik Gabel for their lifetimes without further payment and, in 1662, they are given the complete trade monopoly.

1653   A fort is built at Tinganes to defend the Monopoly buildings.

1658   The *ting* decides not only to finish the fort at Tinganes but also to put the old fort at Skansin on a defensive footing and that 30 soldiers should be stationed there.

1669   Tarnovius writers about the Faroes: *Ferøers Beskrifvelser*. This is the first of a series of descriptions of the Faroes during this century.

1672–3   Royal Commission on Faroese Affairs.

1673   Lucas Debes wrote a book: *Færoæ et Færoa Reserata* (A description of the Faroes and its inhabitants). A fire breaks out in the Tinganes buildings. Nearly all the Monopoly's buildings as well as the *ting*-house are burnt down and the fort's powder-magazine explodes. Dower farms for the widows of ministers are granted.

1677	The fort, Skansin, and part of Tórshavn are destroyed by French pirates.
1688	Christian V's Norwegian Law of 1687 comes into effect in the Faroes as well.
1691	Land and Monopoly laws are enacted.
1698	Individual ownership of sheep is forbidden.
1706	The first and only death penalty carried out under Norwegian law, when a brother and sister are beheaded for incest.
1709–1856	The Royal Trade Monopoly is instituted.
1768	Ryberg sets up a trading company in Tórshavn. Special permission is given him to store foreign goods and to deal in transit goods. The factory was run by the merchant company Rosenmeyer and Floor. They taught the Faroese to salt herring and they were the first to export dried fish from the Faroes.
1776	The secular and church administration was placed under the diocese of Sjælland.
1781–2	Jens Christian Svabo undertook some research in the Faroes and wrote a book: *Indberetning fra en Reise i Færoe 1781–82* (A report on a journey to the Faroes).
1804	Nólsoyar-Páll built the ship *Royndin Fríða* (The beautiful experiment) and was, thereby, the first Faroese since Magnus Heinason to own a ship. The Latin school (set up 1547) is closed down.
1808	The English Captain Baugh attacks Tórshavn and takes Skansin. Later the same year, Baron von Hompesch loots the Monopoly's assets and the Church.
1809	Nólsoyar-Páll disappears at sea, *en route* to the Faroes.
1814	The Treaty of Kiel. The Danish–Norwegian union is dissolved. The Faroes, Iceland and Greenland remain under Danish jurisdiction.
1816	The *ting* is abolished. The Faroes become a Danish county. Commander Löbner is appointed provisional prefect or governor.
1821	The first prefect is appointed (Löbner).
1845	The decree on compulsory schooling. Folk schools are set up.
1846	V. U. Hammershaimb lays the basis for a Faroese script.
1850	The Danish Constitution of 1849 is declared valid for the Faroes, without the consent of the Faroese.

1851	The first general election for a Faroese MP to the Danish Parliament (*Folketinget*). Niels Winther elected.
1852	The Faroese *ting* (*Løgtinget*) is restored but with only advisory functions. Niels Winther gives out the first Faroese political paper *Færingetiðende* (*The Faroese Times*).
1856	The Royal Danish Trade Monopoly is abolished. Free trade is allowed.
1861	A primary school is set up in Tórshavn.
1870	The Faroese Teacher Training College is established.
1872	Sloop fisheries begin; the first sloop is bought from Britain.
1888–9	The Nationalist Movement. The Faroese League is founded.
1899	The Faroese Folk High School is founded.
1905–6	The first political parties, The Unionist (*Sambandsflokkurin*) and the Independence (*Sjálvstýrisflokkurin*) parties, are formed.
1906	The Faroese Telephone Company is established.
1911	*Additions to the suggestions and recommendations of the Faroese Agricultural Commission*: the report on the rationalization of land tenure is published.
1918	The Independence Party wins a majority for the first time.
1923	The law concerning the *Løgting* is changed: the prefect and the dean are no longer members *de jure*; the *Løgting* becomes democratic.
1928	The Social Democratic Party (*Javnaðarflokkurin*) founded in 1925, is represented in the Løgting. The village of Fámjin is the first village to be rationalized as regards land tenure.
1937	The Faroese *Løgting* sets up a new High School.
1938	The debatable Para 7 that general school teaching should be in Danish, is abolished.
1940–5	The Faroes are occupied by British troops.
1940	The Faroese flag is recognized as the national one by the British. The People's party (*Folkaflokkurin*) is founded.
1944	The electoral franchise is extended to 21-year-olds by the *Løgting*.
1945	The British leave an airstrip on Vágar for the Faroese.
1946	A referendum concerning the Faroese political position, *vis-à-vis* Denmark, was held on 14 September. A small majority voted for independence but as this was only a third the electorate it was taken by the Danes that the current

union should continue. The inter-kommunal electricity company, SEV (Streymoy, Eysteroy, Vágar) is set up.

1948   The Home Rule Ordinance came into effect on 1 April. The Republican party (*Tjoðveldisflokkurin*) was founded. The Danish Governor is replaced by a High Commissioner.

1951   The Faroese Fishery Industry Bank (*Sjóvinnubankin*) collapses.

1954   A general strike in the fishing industry.

1955   A Credit Institute, for the fishing fleet, was set up.

1957   Faroese Radio (*Utvarp Føroya*) was founded.

1959   National Insurance law (old-age pensions, etc.) was introduced.

1963   The Faroes become the see of a vice-bishop. The first tunnel is built between Tvøroyri and Hvalba.

1964   A 12-mile fishing limit is announced by the Faroese. The 60 million kroner rolling investment fund for the Faroes is set up by Denmark.

1965   The Faroese Academy (*Fróðskaparsetur Føroya*) is set up by law.

1968   The Faroes join EFTA.

1970   The Faroes are represented on the Nordic Council.

1972   The Faroes leave EFTA with Denmark, but do not join the EEC.

1975   The first Faroese postage stamps are issued.

1976   The fishing limits are now unilaterally extended to 200 miles.

1977   Special fishing agreement reached with the EEC.

1979   The Faroes are represented on NAFO (North-west Atlantic Fisheries Organization) by Denmark.

1982   The Faroes are represented on NEAFO (North-east Atlantic Fisheries Organization) by Denmark.

1983   The Nordic House, for cultural activities, is opened in Tórshavn.

1984   Faroese television (*Sjónvarp Føroya*) begins trial broadcasts, after the suppression of a private television station.

1989   Financial crisis. A new government introduces austerity measures.

Glossary, Spelling and Pronunciation

Glossary

á	river
á	to
átjan	eighteen
átta	eight
av	from
avgreiðslutið	office hours
broytning	change/alteration
bussleiðir	bus routes
bøur	infield
eiði	isthmus
eitt	one
ellivu	eleven
farið verður	it departs
ferðafólk	travellers
ferðamannakort	tourist card
ferðseðlakostnaðir	ticket price
ferðætlan	timetable
ferja	ferry
fimm	five
fímtan	fifteen
fjøruti	forty
flogfar	plane
fraferð	departure
friggjadagur	Friday
fjúrtan	fourteen
fjørd	fjord
fýra	four
fyrrapartur	morning
fyrs	eighty
galdandi	current
gjógv	fissure

glas stova	fine room
grind	pilot whale
grindaboð	warning of approaching pilot whales
gøta	street/road
hagi	outfield
hálvtryss	fifty
hálvfjerðs	seventy
hálvfems	ninety
Havn	Tórshavn
hósdagur	Thursday
hundrað	hundred
hjallur	drying-house
keypa	buy
kostnaður	price
kommune	local authority
koyra	drive
klipfisk	dried, salted cod
kvøld	evening
kvæði	ballads
leygardagur	Saturday
leypur	wooden creel
løgting	parliament
lukket	closed
mánadagur	Monday
mikudagur	Wednesday
múli	promontory
neyst	boathouse
níggju	nine
nítjan	nineteen
ólavsøka	29 July, National Day
opin	open
ókeypis	gratis
roykstova	'smoky-room': the work room
seinasta	last
seinnapartur	afternoon
seks	six
sekstan	sixteen
sigling	sailing
sjey	seven
sjeytjan	seventeen
sjónvarp	television
skerpikjøt	wind-dried mutton
skrivstova	office
sornhús	corn drying-house
stór	large

sund	sound
sunnudag	Sunday
táttur	satirical song
tindur	peak
ting	*ting*/thing/assembly
tjúgu	twenty
tíggjur	ten
tólv	twelve
tretivu	thirty
trettan	thirteen
trøð	outfield enclosure
trý	three
trýss	sixty
tvey	two
tusund	thousand
tyrla	helicopter
týsdagur	Thursday
úr	from
útvarp	radio
vág	bay
vegur	road
við	near
vík	cove
viðmerkningar	notice!
yvirlit	overview/survey

Spelling and pronunciation

1. Faroese has some eight different alphabetical characters to English: á, ð, í, ó, ú, ý, ø, æ: in both lower and upper case.
2. The pronunciation of the different vowels are, roughly:

á	oa	Gáshólmur
á	oh	Ánir
í	uy	Høyvík
ý	uy	fýra
ó	orh	Nólsoy
ó	oe	Gjógv
ú	oo	Húsar
ú	y	fjúrtan
æ	eh	Æðuvík
ø	erh	Trøllanes

3. Other special pronunciations are:

ð	(mute)	Eiði
ll	dl	hjallur
hv	kv	Hvalba
g	v	vegur
g	g	Gøta

4. The stress in Faroese normally falls on the first syllable. For further details regarding grammar and vocabulary you are referred to Lockwood's *An introduction to modern Faroese* and Young's *Faroese–English Dictionary*.

Bibliography

Hjaltason, K. *Færøerne rundt – en guide*, 4th edn. (Skarv, Holte [in Danish] 1988)

Jackson, A. 'Faroese folk-tales (*Folklore* no. 87, 1976) pp. 50–9

Jackson A. 'Faroese fare' in J. Kuper (ed.) *The anthropologists' cookbook* (Routledge and Kegan Paul, London, 1977) pp. 48–51

Jackson, A. 'Socio-economic change in the Faroes' in R. Andersen (ed.) *North Atlantic Maritime Cultures* (Mouton Publishers, The Hague, 1979) pp. 309–26

Jackson, A. 'Migration patterns in the Faroe Islands: Some comparisons with Scotland' in H. Jones (ed.) *Recent migration in Northern Scotland: Pattern, Process, Impact*, North Sea Oil Panel Occasional Paper No. 13 (SSRC, London, 1982) pp. 130–40

Jackson, A. 'Northern Europe: The Faroes' in *The Atlas of Mankind* (Mitchell Beazley, London, 1982) pp. 68–9

Jackson, A. 'An introduction to the Faroes', Northern Studies, Edinburgh no. 20, 1984, pp. 1–4

Jackson, A. 'Demographic change in the Faroes' *8th International Seminar on Marginal Regions* (Galway, 1986) pp. 117–153

Jackson, A. 'Symbolic heroes: The construction of Faroese identity': *9th International Seminar on Marginal Regions* (Belfast, 1988) pp. 323–336

Jackson A. 'Art for Art's sake or for the sake of nationalism?' *10th International Seminar on Marginal Regions* (Halifax, Nova Scotia, 1990)

Klindt-Jensen, O. *A history of Scandinavian Archaeology* (Thames and Hudson, London, 1973)

Lockwood, W. B. *The Faroese bird names* (Munksgaard, Copenhagen, 1961)

Lockwood, W. B. *An introduction to modern Faroese* (Munksgaard, Copenhagen, 1964)

Nagel. *Scandinavia* (Nagel, Geneva, 1959)

Nordal, J. (ed.) *Iceland 874–1974* (Central Bank, Reykjavík, 1975)

Torsteinsson, A. *Tinganes – Tórshavn* (Føroya Landstýri, Tórshavn, 1986)

Trap, J. P. *Danmark: Færøerne, XIII*, 5th edn. (Gads, Copenhagen [in Danish], 1968)

West, J. *Faroe: The emergence of a nation* (Hurst, London, 1972)

Williamson, K. *The Atlantic Islands*, 2nd edn. (Routledge and Kegan Paul, London, 1970)

Young, G. V. C. and Clewer, C. R. *The Faroese Saga* (Føroyar Skúlabókagrunnir, Tórshavn, 1973)

Young, G. V. C. and Clewer, C. R. *Faroese–English Dictionary* (Manx-Svensk, Peel, Isle of Man, 1985)

Index

*Ferry boat
Page references given in **bold numbers** refer to the most important descriptions of particular places.